I0842500

Welcome to "Bullshit/Not Bullshit," your ultimate coffee table companion and conversation starter! In a world teeming with information, it can be a wild ride trying to separate the nuggets of truth from the piles of nonsense. This book is here to make that ride both fun and enlightening.

Think of "Bullshit/Not Bullshit" as the perfect game for gatherings, sparking debates and laughter as you and your friends dive into the intriguing world of commonly held beliefs. Is that old wives' tale your grandmother swore by actually true? Can eating carrots really improve your eyesight? We're here to explore these questions and more, with a mix of curiosity and a healthy dose of skepticism.

This book isn't just about busting myths — it's about enjoying the journey of discovery. Each page presents you with a claim, inviting you to ponder, discuss, and guess whether it's legit or a load of baloney. It's a playful way to challenge what you think you know and to learn something new in the process.

So, grab your favorite drink, gather your friends, and get ready for some spirited discussions. "Bullshit/Not Bullshit" is here to entertain, educate, and keep you guessing. Let the fun begin!

Table Of Contents

Alcohol

Vodka is traditionally made from potatoes.

Answer: Bullshit - Most vodka is distilled from fermented grains such as corn, rye, or wheat. Potatoes are used in some vodka production, but they are not the primary source.

Beer is older than wine in human history.

Answer: Not Bullshit - Beer is believed to be older than wine in human history, with evidence of beer production dating back at least 7,000 years, possibly predating wine.

Tequila is made from any kind of agave plant.

Answer: Bullshit - Tequila must be made from the blue agave plant, specifically. Other types of agave plants are not used in making authentic tequila.

Bonus Fact: The shortest war in history was the Anglo-Zanzibar War of 1896, lasting between 38 and 45 minutes.

Bourbon can only be made in Kentucky.

Answer: Bullshit - Bourbon can be produced anywhere in the United States. The designation of bourbon is based on ingredients, process, and aging, not location.

Absinthe is hallucinogenic.

Answer: Bullshit - Absinthe is not hallucinogenic. The myth likely stems from the presence of thujone in wormwood, an ingredient in absinthe, but the levels of thujone are too low to have hallucinogenic effects.

A "proof" of alcohol is twice its percentage of alcohol by volume (ABV).

Answer: Not Bullshit - In the United States, the proof of an alcoholic beverage is indeed twice its ABV.

Bonus Fact: A day on Venus is longer than a year on Venus due to its slow rotation.

Champagne can only be produced in the Champagne region of France.

Answer: Not Bullshit - To be legally called Champagne, the sparkling wine must originate from the Champagne region of France and adhere to specific production rules. In other parts of the world, sparkling wine is known by different names: Cava (Spain), Prosecco (Italy), Sekt (Germany), Crémant (various regions in France outside Champagne), Espumante (Portugal), Sparkling Wine (general term in English-speaking countries like the U.S.).

Sake is a type of beer.

Answer: Bullshit - Sake, often called Japanese rice wine, is more similar to wine than beer in its production process, as it involves fermenting polished rice.

Bonus Fact: Cleopatra was closer in time to the moon landing than to the construction of the Great Pyramid of Giza.

Whiskey and whisky are the same thing.

Answer: Bullshit - The spelling indicates the country of origin. "Whiskey" is used by countries with an 'e' in their names (like the United States and Ireland), while "whisky" is used by countries without an 'e' (like Scotland and Canada).

The worm in a bottle of mezcal is a traditional feature from its origin.

Answer: Bullshit - The worm in the bottle of mezcal is more of a marketing gimmick than a traditional feature, starting in the mid-20th century and not typically part of authentic mezcal production.

All Scotch is whisky, but not all whisky is Scotch.

Answer: Not Bullshit - Scotch refers specifically to whisky made in Scotland. Whisky made in other regions cannot legally be called Scotch.

Drinking alcohol kills brain cells.

Answer: Bullshit - While excessive alcohol use can damage the brain, moderate consumption does not kill brain cells. It can, however, impair communication between neurons.

Margaritas are a traditional Mexican cocktail.

Answer: Bullshit - The Margarita's origins are debated, but many believe it was actually invented by Americans. It is more of a modern cocktail than a traditional Mexican one.

Gin is made from juniper berries.

Answer: Not Bullshit - The primary flavor of gin comes from juniper berries, which is a key ingredient in its distillation process.

Red wine must be served at room temperature.

Answer: Bullshit - The ideal serving temperature for red wine is slightly below room temperature, around 15-18°C (60-65°F).

The term 'proof' for alcohol strength comes from a 16th-century English tax law.

Answer: Not Bullshit - The term 'proof' originated from a 16th-century English tax law where spirits had to be 'proven' to be above a certain strength to be taxed.

Vermouth is a type of beer.

Answer: Bullshit - Vermouth is actually a type of aromatized wine, flavored with various botanicals.

Only women drank beer in ancient Egypt.

Answer: Bullshit - In ancient Egypt, both men and women drank beer, and it was a common part of their daily diet.

The term 'spirits' for distilled beverages comes from medieval alchemy.

Answer: Not Bullshit - The term 'spirits' for distilled beverages is believed to come from medieval alchemy, where distillation was thought to release the 'spirit' of the liquid.

The oldest known recipe in the world is for beer.

Answer: Not Bullshit - The oldest known recipe in the world is indeed for beer, dating back to ancient Sumeria.

Distilled spirits can spoil if they are left open.

Answer: Bullshit - Distilled spirits like whiskey, vodka, and rum do not spoil easily, even if left open, due to their high alcohol content.

Bonus Fact: Oxford University is older than the Aztec Empire, with teaching starting in 1096, while the Aztec Empire was founded in 1428.

Beer was not considered an alcoholic beverage in Russia until 2011.

Answer: Not Bullshit - Beer was classified as a foodstuff and not an alcoholic beverage in Russia until 2011. This was due to a legal loophole that classified any beverage with less than 10% alcohol content as a foodstuff. It wasn't until 2011 that legislation was passed to reclassify beer as an alcoholic beverage, allowing for more regulation on its sale and consumption.

The first recorded instance of a hangover cure was in ancient Assyria.

Answer: Not Bullshit - The ancient Assyrians had a hangover cure that included ground bird beaks and myrrh. This concoction was believed to help alleviate the symptoms of a hangover. The Assyrians, like many ancient civilizations, had a deep understanding of herbal remedies and believed that specific combinations of ingredients could help restore balance to the body after excessive drinking.**

Bonus Fact: Hot water can freeze faster than cold water under certain conditions, a phenomenon known as the Mpemba effect.

Guinness beer is black.

Answer: Bullshit - Although Guinness is often thought to be black, it's actually a very deep ruby red. This color comes from the way the malted barley is roasted, similar to how coffee beans are roasted. The dark color and rich flavor have led many to describe it as black, but when held up to the light, its true color is revealed.

Wine is older than beer in human history.

Answer: Bullshit - Beer is believed to be older than wine in human history, with evidence of beer dating back further than wine.

In medieval Europe, beer was often safer to drink than water.

Answer: Not Bullshit - In medieval Europe, the process of brewing beer killed many pathogens, making it safer to drink than water, which was often contaminated.

A standard glass of wine has more alcohol than a standard beer.

Answer: Bullshit - Generally, a standard glass of wine has about the same amount of alcohol as a standard beer, depending on the specific types and serving sizes.

Prohibition in the United States completely stopped the production and consumption of alcohol.

Answer: Bullshit - Prohibition in the United States (1920-1933) did not completely stop the production and consumption of alcohol. Illegal production and speakeasies were common, and some alcohol was legally allowed for medicinal purposes.

Bonus Fact: The Eiffel Tower can grow more than 6 inches during hot weather due to thermal expansion.

In Scotland, there is a barrel of whisky that has been aging since the 18th century.

Answer: Bullshit - While Scotland is renowned for its long-aged whiskies, there is no known barrel that has been aging since the 18th century. The process of aging whisky over such a long period would result in most of the liquid being lost to evaporation, known as the "angel's share."

The color of the wine is determined by the grape's skin, not its juice.

Answer: Not Bullshit - The color of wine is primarily determined by the skin of the grapes. The juice from most purple grapes is actually greenish-white; the red color in wines like Cabernet Sauvignon and Merlot is achieved by leaving the crushed grape skins in contact with the juice for a period of time during fermentation.

Bonus Fact: There are more possible iterations of a game of chess than there are atoms in the known universe.

Guinness Stout was the result of a burnt batch of beer.

Answer: Not Bullshit - (Mostly) - The story goes that Arthur Guinness, the founder of the Guinness brewery, was experimenting with a batch of beer when he accidentally over-roasted the barley. This mistake resulted in a much darker and richer beer, which eventually became the signature style for Guinness Stout.

Bonus Fact: Bananas are naturally radioactive because they contain potassium-40, a radioactive isotope of potassium.

Animals

Sharks can live for over 400 years.

Answer: Not Bullshit - Some species of sharks, like the Greenland shark, have been found to live for centuries, with estimates of their lifespan exceeding 400 years.

Cats have fewer toes on their back paws.

Answer: Not Bullshit - Cats typically have five toes on their front paws and four toes on their back paws.

Koalas have human-like fingerprints.

Answer: Not Bullshit - Koalas have fingerprints that are remarkably similar to human fingerprints, so much so that they can be indistinguishable under a microscope.

The male seahorse gives birth to its young.

Answer: Not Bullshit - Male seahorses are equipped with a pouch where females deposit eggs. The male then fertilizes and carries the eggs until they hatch and are released into the water.

Dolphins sleep with one eye open.

Answer: Not Bullshit - Dolphins sleep with one half of their brain at a time, allowing one eye to remain open to stay alert for predators and surface for air.

Peacock feathers are naturally colorful.

Answer: Bullshit - The vibrant colors of a peacock's feathers are not due to pigment but are structural, resulting from the reflection and refraction of light due to the microscopic structure of the feathers.

Butterflies taste with their feet.

Answer: Not Bullshit - Butterflies have taste receptors on their feet to help them find their host plants and locate nectar.

Camels store water in their humps.

Answer: Bullshit - Camel humps do not store water; they store fat, which can provide energy when food and water are scarce.

Rabbits and hares are the same species.

Answer: Bullshit - Although they look similar and are often confused, rabbits and hares are different species with distinct behaviors and physical characteristics.

An ostrich's eye is bigger than its brain.

Answer: Not Bullshit - The eyes of an ostrich are indeed larger than its brain, which is one of the reasons for their excellent eyesight.

Hummingbirds are the only birds that can fly backwards.

Answer: Not Bullshit - Hummingbirds have the unique ability to fly in any direction, including backwards, thanks to their wing structure.

A group of crows is called a 'murder.'

Answer: Not Bullshit - A group of crows is indeed referred to as a 'murder.' This term has been used since at least the 15th century and likely stems from the crow's association with death and dark omens in folklore and mythology. Crows are scavengers often seen around sites of death, which may have contributed to the macabre term. Additionally, crows are highly intelligent birds known for their complex social behaviors, and the term 'murder' poetically reflects their mysterious and somewhat eerie nature.

All tarantulas are deadly to humans.

Answer: Bullshit - While tarantulas are venomous, their venom is not deadly to humans except in extremely rare allergic reactions.

Crocodiles can grow new teeth to replace the old ones throughout their lives.

Answer: Not Bullshit - Crocodiles have a continuous tooth replacement cycle, allowing them to grow new teeth to replace lost or worn ones.

The tongue of a blue whale is as heavy as an elephant.

Answer: Not Bullshit - The tongue of a blue whale can weigh as much as an elephant, highlighting the massive size of these marine mammals.

Bonus Fact: The shortest commercial flight in the world lasts just 57 seconds between the Scottish islands of Westray and Papa Westray.

Snakes can blink.

Answer: Bullshit - Snakes do not have eyelids, so they cannot blink. Instead, they have a transparent scale called a spectacle that covers and protects their eyes.

Frogs drink water through their skin.

Answer: Not Bullshit - Frogs absorb water through their skin in an area known as the 'drinking patch' located on their belly and the underside of their thighs.

Polar bears have white fur.

Answer: Bullshit - Polar bear fur is actually transparent and hollow; it appears white because it reflects light.

Bonus Fact: Sharks have existed for about 400 million years, whereas trees have been around for around 350 million years.

Goldfish have a three-second memory.

Answer: Bullshit - Goldfish have been shown to have a memory span of several months, not just a few seconds.

The cheetah is the only cat that cannot retract its claws.

Answer: Not Bullshit - The cheetah's claws are semi-retractable and help provide traction during high-speed chases.

A cow's moo can have a regional accent.

Answer: Not Bullshit - Studies suggest that cows' moos can vary in accent depending on the region they are from, much like human accents.

Bonus Fact: Mantis shrimp have the most complex eyes, with 16 color receptors compared to humans' three, allowing them to see ultraviolet light.

Turtles can breathe through their butts.

Answer: Not Bullshit - Some turtle species can perform a form of respiration through their cloaca, an orifice used for excretion and reproduction, allowing them to stay underwater for longer periods.

Elephants are the only mammals that can't jump.

Answer: Not Bullshit - Due to their size and leg structure, elephants are indeed the only mammals that cannot jump.

A giraffe's spots are unique like human fingerprints.

Answer: Not Bullshit - No two giraffes have exactly the same pattern of spots, making each giraffe's coat unique.

Bonus Fact: Some turtles can breathe through their butts, a process known as cloacal respiration.

Wolves howl at the moon.

Answer: Bullshit - Wolves do not howl at the moon. Howling is a form of communication among wolves, used to regroup or signal their location, regardless of the moon's presence.

Bonus Fact: Cows form strong social bonds and can become stressed when separated from their preferred partner.

Art & Literature

Vincent van Gogh sold only one painting during his lifetime.

Answer: Not Bullshit - Van Gogh sold very few paintings during his lifetime, with only one known sale, "The Red Vineyard."

Shakespeare invented the game of chess.

Answer: Bullshit - Chess predates Shakespeare by several centuries, originating in India around the 6th century.

The Mona Lisa has no eyebrows.

Answer: Not Bullshit - The Mona Lisa appears to have no visible eyebrows, which was a common fashion in the Renaissance period. It's also possible they have faded over time.

J.K. Rowling, The author of the Harry Potter book series, was the first person to become a billionaire by writing books.

Answer: Not Bullshit - J.K. Rowling is considered the first author to become a billionaire from book writing, largely thanks to the Harry Potter series.

The 'Last Supper' by Leonardo da Vinci includes a hidden musical score.

Answer: Bullshit - There's no credible evidence to support the claim that Leonardo da Vinci included a hidden musical score in 'The Last Supper.'

The Statue of Liberty was a gift from France to the USA.

Answer: Not Bullshit - The Statue of Liberty was indeed a gift from France to the United States, commemorating the centennial of American independence.

J.R.R. Tolkien created over ten languages.

Answer: Not Bullshit - J.R.R. Tolkien was a linguist and created several languages, including Elvish languages, for his Middle-earth stories.

Edgar Allan Poe married his 13-year-old cousin.

Answer: Not Bullshit - Edgar Allan Poe married his cousin Virginia Clemm when she was 13 and he was 27.

The original title of Jane Austen's 'Pride and Prejudice' was 'First Impressions.'

Answer: Not Bullshit - Jane Austen's 'Pride and Prejudice' was originally titled 'First Impressions' before it was revised and published under its current title.

Michelangelo painted the ceiling of the Sistine Chapel lying on his back.

Answer: Bullshit - Michelangelo painted the Sistine Chapel ceiling standing up, using a specially designed scaffold.

The character Sherlock Holmes never actually says "Elementary, my dear Watson" in any of the original stories.

Answer: Not Bullshit - The phrase "Elementary, my dear Watson" is not found in the original Sherlock Holmes stories by Arthur Conan Doyle.

'Moby-Dick' was a commercial success during Herman Melville's lifetime.

Answer: Bullshit - 'Moby-Dick' was not a commercial success during Melville's lifetime and only gained significant acclaim posthumously.

The Louvre was originally constructed as a museum.

Answer: Bullshit - The Louvre was originally built as a fortress in the late 12th century and later converted into a royal palace before becoming a museum.

The 'Twilight' series was originally written as 'Harry Potter' fan fiction.

Answer: Bullshit - The 'Twilight' series by Stephenie Meyer was not originally 'Harry Potter' fan fiction, though 'Fifty Shades of Grey' by E.L. James began as 'Twilight' fan fiction.

George Orwell fought in the Spanish Civil War.

Answer: Not Bullshit - George Orwell did indeed fight in the Spanish Civil War, an experience he wrote about in 'Homage to Catalonia.'

Charles Dickens always wrote his novels by hand.

Answer: Not Bullshit - Charles Dickens wrote his novels by hand, as typewriters were not yet commonly used during his time.

The 'Mona Lisa' was stolen from the Louvre in 1911 and missing for several years.

Answer: Not Bullshit - The 'Mona Lisa' was indeed stolen from the Louvre in 1911 and was missing for two years before being recovered. Pablo Picasso was a suspect.

Salvador Dalí designed the Chupa Chups logo.

Answer: Not Bullshit - Salvador Dalí did design the logo for Chupa Chups, the Spanish lollipop company.

Bonus Fact: Wombats poop cubes, which helps their feces stay in place and mark their territory.

Hans Christian Andersen's original version of 'The Little Mermaid' has a happy ending.

Answer: Bullshit - The original version of 'The Little Mermaid' by Hans Christian Andersen has a tragic ending, quite different from the popular Disney adaptation.

The character Dracula was inspired by Vlad the Impaler.

Answer: Not Bullshit - Bram Stoker's character Dracula was indeed inspired by the historical figure Vlad the Impaler.

Leonardo da Vinci could write with one hand and draw with the other at the same time.

Answer: Not Bullshit - Leonardo da Vinci was ambidextrous and is reported to have been able to write with one hand while drawing with the other.

Bonus Fact: Sloths can hold their breath for up to 40 minutes, while dolphins need to surface for air every 10 minutes.

Despite inventing the Theory of Relativity, Einstein was a terrible math student.

Answer: Bullshit - The rumor that Einstein "flunked a math test" came from a semi-true story where he failed a high school entrance exam. He did fine on the math portion, but it was the essay section that tripped him up since the questions were written in French, a language he didn't fully understand.

Agatha Christie disappeared for ten days and never remembered or explained what happened.

Answer: Not Bullshit - Agatha Christie did disappear for eleven days in 1926, and the event remains shrouded in mystery with no clear explanation.

Frankenstein is the name of the monster in Mary Shelley's novel.

Answer: Bullshit - In Mary Shelley's novel, Frankenstein is the name of the scientist, not the monster. The monster is commonly referred to as "Frankenstein's monster."

The first ever grammy in the "Rap" category was won by will smith and DJ jazzy Jeff.

Answer: Not Bullshit - "Parents just don't understand" was the first song to win a Grammy in the rap category"

Dr. Seuss once included the word "contraceptive" to make sure that his publisher was paying attention to what he wrote.

Answer: Not Bullshit - The original draft of the book "Hop on Pop contains these lines: 'When I read, I am smart / I always cut whole words apart. / Con Stan Tin O Ple, Tim Buk Too / Con Tra Cep Tive, Kan Ga Roo.' We're pleased to report that the publisher, Bennett Cerf, was paying attention, and this line was removed.

There is a broken chain at the foot of the Statue of Liberty that can only be seen from an aerial view.

Answer: Not Bullshit – The chain was made by the creator of the statue (a firm backer of Abraham Lincoln) as a sign of the end of all forms of servitude.

Hall and Oates met while ducking gunfire

Answer: Not Bullshit – Jerry Bishop, a popular DJ at the time promoted a dance event where both Hall and Oates who were in separate bands were invited. When gunfire broke out, the two were hiding together.

Sophia Stewart wrote books in the 1970's that were later stolen by Warner Brosto create the Terminator movies 1-4 and the Matrix 1 & 2

Answer: Bullshit – Ms. Stewart did make such accusations, but her trial was dismissed due to lack of evidence.

Famous Playwright Tennessee Williams died of a drug overdose.

Answer: Bullshit (sort of) – Williams met his end by choking on a bottle cap, which came from the bottle that housed his barbiturates.

Bonus Fact: Goosebumps are a reflex left over from our ancestors who had more body hair, making them look bigger and scarier when it was raised.

Economics & Business

Bitcoin was the first digital currency.

Answer: Not Bullshit - Bitcoin, created in 2009, is widely recognized as the first decentralized digital currency or cryptocurrency.

The New York Stock Exchange is the largest stock exchange in the world by market capitalization.

Answer: Not Bullshit - The New York Stock Exchange (NYSE) is indeed the largest stock exchange in the world by total market capitalization of its listed companies.

Starbucks was named after a character in Herman Melville's 'Moby Dick.'

Answer: Not Bullshit - Starbucks was named after the first mate in Melville's novel, Starbuck.

Bonus Fact: The arteries of a blue whale are so large that a small child could swim through them.

The concept of the 'invisible hand' was introduced by Karl Marx.

Answer: Bullshit - The concept of the 'invisible hand,' suggesting that self-interested behavior can lead to positive economic outcomes, was introduced by Adam Smith, not Karl Marx.

Bill Gates dropped out of college to start Microsoft.

Answer: Not Bullshit - Bill Gates did drop out of Harvard University to found Microsoft with Paul Allen.

McDonald's once made bubblegum-flavored broccoli.

Answer: Not Bullshit - McDonald's tested bubblegum-flavored broccoli as a way to make vegetables more appealing to children, but it was not well-received.

Bonus Fact: Scotland's national animal is the unicorn, a mythical creature that has been a symbol of the country for centuries.

The first product to have a barcode was Wrigley's gum.

Answer: Not Bullshit - The first product scanned using a Universal Product Code (UPC) was a pack of Wrigley's chewing gum in 1974.

A group of economists won the Nobel Prize for creating the game Monopoly.

Answer: Bullshit - The game Monopoly was not created by economists, nor has anyone won a Nobel Prize for its creation. It was designed by Lizzie Magie and later popularized by Charles Darrow.

Amazon started as an online bookstore.

Answer: Not Bullshit - Amazon.com began in a garage as an online bookstore before expanding into a wide variety of other products.

The 'Laffer Curve' illustrates the relationship between tax rates and government revenue.

Answer: Not Bullshit - The Laffer Curve, named after economist Arthur Laffer, theorizes the relationship between tax rates and the amount of tax revenue collected by governments.

Walt Disney holds the patent for credit cards.

Answer: Bullshit - Walt Disney did not hold the patent for credit cards. The concept of credit cards predates his era, with various forms of credit tokens used historically.

'Black Friday' is named so because it is the day retailers' finances move from 'the red' into 'the black.'

Answer: Not Bullshit - The term "Black Friday" originally referred to the day when retailers began to turn a profit for the year, or move from "the red" into "the black."

The logo of Apple Inc. is a tribute to Alan Turing.

Answer: Bullshit - The Apple logo was not designed as a tribute to Alan Turing. The bitten apple design was chosen for scale distinction, so it wouldn't be confused with a cherry.

Henry Ford invented the automobile.

Answer: Bullshit - Henry Ford did not invent the automobile; he revolutionized its production with assembly line manufacturing, making cars more affordable. Karl Benz is often credited with creating the first true automobile, Benz patented his Benz Patent-Motorwagen in 1886. This vehicle was powered by an internal combustion engine and is considered the first practical automobile. Though there were several contributors.

Bonus Fact: Humans are the only animals that blush and are also believed to be the only species that feels embarrassment.

The richest person in history was John D. Rockefeller.

Answer: Bullshit - While John D. Rockefeller was immensely wealthy, Mansa Musa, the 14th-century emperor of the Mali Empire, is often considered the richest person in history.

Coca-Cola originally contained cocaine.

Answer: Not Bullshit - In its early formulation, Coca-Cola did contain a small amount of cocaine, derived from coca leaves, until it was removed in the early 20th century. The company still imports Coca leaves for its recipe, but the stimulant is removed.

The term 'Blue Chip' in the stock market comes from the color of high-value chips in poker.

Answer: Not Bullshit - In the stock market, "blue chip" stocks are named after the blue chips in poker, which are typically the highest value.

IKEA names its furniture products after Swedish towns.

Answer: Bullshit - IKEA product names are based on a specific naming system involving Swedish words, names of places, but not limited to towns, and other categories.

The Great Depression started with the stock market crash of 1929.

Answer: Not Bullshit - The Great Depression began after the stock market crash of October 1929, which sent Wall Street into a panic and wiped out millions of investors.

Google was originally called 'BackRub.'

Answer: Not Bullshit - Google's original name was indeed 'BackRub,' named for its analysis of the web's "back links."

Forbes is a publicly-traded company.

Answer: Bullshit - Forbes is a privately-held media company, known for its financial news and rankings.

Samsung started as a grocery trading store.

Answer: Not Bullshit - Samsung began as a small trading company in 1938, dealing in groceries and making noodles.

The term 'NASDAQ' stands for National Association of Securities Dealers Automated Quotations.

Answer: Not Bullshit - NASDAQ does stand for National Association of Securities Dealers Automated Quotations.

The first paper money was created in ancient Rome.

Answer: Bullshit - The first known use of paper money was in China during the Tang dynasty in the 7th century.

Bitcoin's creator, Satoshi Nakamoto, is a pseudonym, and their real identity is known.

Answer: Bullshit - The true identity of Satoshi Nakamoto, the creator of Bitcoin, remains unknown and is one of the great mysteries in the world of cryptocurrency.

OPEC stands for Organization of Petroleum Exporting Countries.

Answer: Not Bullshit - OPEC does stand for the Organization of Petroleum Exporting Countries, an intergovernmental organization of oil-exporting nations.

Enron's collapse led to the creation of the Sarbanes-Oxley Act.

Answer: Not Bullshit - The Sarbanes-Oxley Act was enacted in response to several major corporate and accounting scandals, including those of Enron and WorldCom.

The 'pink tax' refers to an actual tax imposed on women's products.

Answer: Bullshit - The 'pink tax' is not an actual tax, but a term used to describe the price discrepancy where products marketed towards women are often more expensive than men's.

The first credit card was introduced in the 1950s.

Answer: Not Bullshit - The first credit card, Diners Club, was introduced in 1950.

'Ponzi scheme' is named after a notorious Italian banker.

Answer: Not Bullshit - The term 'Ponzi scheme' is named after Charles Ponzi, who became infamous for using this fraudulent investment method in the early 20th century.

Bonus Fact: A group of flamingos is called a "flamboyance."

Food & Cooking

Adding salt to water increases the boiling point, making it cook faster.

Answer: Bullshit - while salt does raise the boiling point of water, the effect is minimal and does not significantly decrease cooking time.

Sushi means 'raw fish'.

Answer: Bullshit - 'Sushi' actually refers to vinegar rice, often accompanied by raw fish or other toppings, but the term itself does not mean raw fish.

Microwaving food destroys its nutrients.

Answer: Bullshit - Microwaving does not destroy more nutrients than other forms of cooking; in some cases, it may preserve nutrients better due to shorter cooking times.

Eating carrots improves your night vision.

Answer: Bullshit - While carrots are high in Vitamin A, which is good for eye health, they do not improve night vision to any significant extent. This myth stems from British propaganda during World War II.

You should wash mushrooms before cooking.

Answer: Not Bullshit - It's advisable to wash mushrooms to remove dirt and debris, but they should be cleaned gently and cooked soon after to prevent them from becoming soggy.

An apple a day keeps the doctor away.

Answer: Bullshit - While apples are healthy and provide various nutrients, eating them alone is not sufficient to guarantee overall health or avoid doctor visits.

MSG (monosodium glutamate) is a harmful chemical additive.

Answer: Bullshit - MSG is a flavor enhancer and, despite common misconceptions, numerous studies have shown that it is safe for consumption for the majority of people.

Cooking vegetables always reduces their nutritional value.

Answer: Bullshit - While cooking can reduce certain nutrients in vegetables, it can also make others more bioavailable, such as lycopene in tomatoes and beta-carotene in carrots.

Honey never spoils.

Answer: Not Bullshit - Due to its low moisture content and high acidity, honey can remain edible for an incredibly long time, even thousands of years.

Frozen vegetables are less nutritious than fresh ones.

Answer: Bullshit - Frozen vegetables can be just as nutritious as fresh ones, sometimes even more so, as they are often frozen shortly after harvesting, preserving their nutrients.

Chocolate causes acne.

Answer: Bullshit - There is no scientific evidence that chocolate directly causes acne. However, a high sugar and high fat diet can contribute to acne for some people.

Decaf coffee is completely caffeine-free.

Answer: Bullshit - Decaffeinated coffee still contains small amounts of caffeine, although much less than regular coffee.

Bonus Fact: Fred Baur, the inventor of the Pringles can, had his ashes buried in one.

Chewing gum takes seven years to digest if swallowed.

Answer: Bullshit - Swallowed gum does not stay in the stomach; it passes through the digestive system relatively intact and is excreted.

Alcohol cooks off completely when used in cooking.

Answer: Bullshit - While some alcohol does evaporate during cooking, a percentage typically remains, depending on cooking method, time, and type of alcohol.

Using metal knives to cut lettuce causes it to brown faster.

Answer: Not Bullshit - Metal knives can react with the acids in lettuce, causing it to brown more quickly. Using a plastic or ceramic knife can lessen this effect.

Red wine should be served at room temperature.

Answer: Bullshit - 'Room temperature' advice originates from a time before central heating. Red wine is often best served slightly cooler, around 15-18°C (60-65°F).

Eating spicy food can cause ulcers.

Answer: Bullshit - Spicy food may irritate existing ulcers but it does not cause them. Most ulcers are caused by bacteria or certain medications, like NSAIDs.

Raw oysters are still alive when you eat them.

Answer: Not Bullshit - Raw oysters are often still alive when eaten, as they deteriorate quickly once they die.

Bonus Fact: Edible honey has been found in ancient Egyptian tombs, demonstrating that honey never spoils.

White chocolate is chocolate.

Answer: Bullshit - White chocolate does not contain cocoa solids, only cocoa butter, so it is not chocolate in the traditional sense.

Brown eggs are more nutritious than white eggs.

Answer: Bullshit - The color of the eggshell is determined by the breed of the hen and does not affect the nutritional value or taste of the egg.

Coffee is made from beans.

Answer: Bullshit - Coffee is made from the seeds of the coffee cherry, which are commonly referred to as beans due to their resemblance.

Bonus Fact: A bolt of lightning is five times hotter than the sun.

Adding oil to pasta water prevents the pasta from sticking.

Answer: Bullshit - Adding oil to pasta water does not prevent sticking; it can actually prevent sauce from adhering to the pasta. Stirring the pasta is a better way to prevent sticking.

Spinach is high in iron.

Answer: Not Bullshit - Spinach is indeed a good source of iron, but not as high as once believed due to a decimal error in an early nutritional study.

Eating too much sugar causes diabetes.

Answer: Bullshit - While excessive sugar consumption is associated with obesity, a risk factor for type 2 diabetes, eating sugar in itself does not directly cause diabetes.

A vegetarian diet does not provide enough protein for humans.

Answer: Bullshit - A well-planned vegetarian diet can provide all the necessary protein. Many plant-based foods are rich in protein.

You should drink at least eight glasses of water a day.

Answer: Bullshit - The amount of water a person needs varies greatly and can be met through various sources, not just drinking water.

All natural flavors are healthier than artificial flavors.

Answer: Bullshit - 'Natural' does not necessarily mean healthier. Natural flavors come from plant or animal sources, but their health effects depend on their specific composition.

Lobsters scream when boiled alive.

Answer: Bullshit - Lobsters don't have vocal cords to scream. The sound heard is air escaping from their shells.

Eating fish makes you smarter.

Answer: Not Bullshit - Fish are high in omega-3 fatty acids, which are beneficial for brain health. However, eating fish alone doesn't guarantee improved intelligence.

Raw and unprocessed foods are always healthier.

Answer: Bullshit - While raw and unprocessed foods can be part of a healthy diet, some foods are more nutritious or safe to eat when cooked.

Bonus Fact: Ketchup was once sold as medicine in the 1830s, marketed as a cure for indigestion.

Geography & Travel

The Sahara Desert is the largest desert in the world.

Answer: Bullshit - The largest desert is actually Antarctica. Deserts are defined by dryness, not just by sand, and Antarctica is the driest and largest desert.

Istanbul is the only city in the world located on two continents.

Answer: Not Bullshit - Istanbul straddles both Europe and Asia, divided by the Bosporus Strait.

Bonus Fact: A single day on Mercury (sunrise to sunrise) lasts about 176 Earth days.

**The Great Barrier Reef is the only living
structure visible from space.**

Answer: Bullshit - While the Great Barrier Reef
is the largest living structure and can be seen
from space, it's not the only one. Other human-
made structures like the Great Wall of China
are also visible.
Other natural formations, such as large forests
and dense vegetation areas, can also be seen
from space. Additionally, certain man-made
structures, like city lights and large agricultural
fields, are visible as well.

**Canada has the longest coastline of any
country in the world.**

Answer: Not Bullshit - Canada does have the
longest coastline of any country, stretching
over 202,080 kilometers (125,567 miles).

Mount Everest grows 4 inches every year.

Answer: Bullshit - Mount Everest grows approximately 4 mm (not inches) annually due to tectonic movements.

Venice is slowly sinking each year.

Answer: Not Bullshit - Venice is indeed sinking at a rate of about 1-2 millimeters per year, compounded by the rising sea levels.

The Amazon River is the longest river in the world.

Answer: Bullshit - While the Amazon is the largest river by discharge volume of water, the Nile River is generally recognized as the longest.

Australia is wider than the moon.

Answer: Not Bullshit - Australia's diameter is about 4,000 km, while the moon's diameter is about 3,474 km, making Australia wider.

There are more pyramids in Sudan than in Egypt.

Answer: Not Bullshit - Sudan has more than 200 pyramids, which is more than in Egypt, though Egypt's are larger and more famous.

The Trans-Siberian Railway is the longest railway in the world.

Answer: Not Bullshit - Spanning over 9,289 kilometers (5,772 miles), the Trans-Siberian Railway is indeed the longest railway line in the world.

Switzerland has no official capital city.

Answer: Bullshit - Bern is the de facto capital of Switzerland, serving as the seat of the federal government.

Alaska is the easternmost and westernmost state in the USA.

Answer: Not Bullshit - Due to the Aleutian Islands stretching across the 180th meridian, Alaska is both the easternmost and westernmost state in the USA.

The Dead Sea is the lowest point on Earth.

Answer: Not Bullshit - The surface and shores of the Dead Sea are the Earth's lowest elevation on land, at 430.5 meters (1,412 feet) below sea level.

The Eiffel Tower was originally intended for Barcelona, Spain, but was rejected.

Answer: Not Bullshit - The design was indeed initially proposed for Barcelona but was rejected. It was then submitted to Paris and constructed for the 1889 Exposition Universelle.

There's a city named Rome on every continent.

Answer: Bullshit - While there are cities named Rome or similar in several continents, there is not one on every continent (e.g., Antarctica).

Africa is the hottest continent on Earth.

Answer: Not Bullshit - Due to its geographical location around the equator, Africa is considered the hottest continent on average.

Lake Baikal in Russia is the deepest lake in the world.

Answer: Not Bullshit - Lake Baikal, located in Siberia, is the world's deepest and oldest freshwater lake, reaching depths of 1,642 meters (5,387 feet).

Bonus Fact: The arteries of a blue whale are so large that a small child could swim through them.

Mount Kilimanjaro is the tallest mountain in the world.

Answer: Bullshit - Mount Kilimanjaro is the tallest mountain in Africa, but Mount Everest is the tallest in the world.

The Leaning Tower of Pisa is the furthest leaning man-made tower in the world.

Answer: Bullshit - While famous for its tilt, the Leaning Tower of Pisa is not the world's furthest leaning man-made tower. The Capital Gate in Abu Dhabi holds the Guinness World Record for the world's furthest leaning man-made tower.

The city of Timbuktu is fictional.

Answer: Bullshit - Timbuktu is a real city in Mali, historically significant as a trade hub and center of Islamic culture.

Bonus Fact: Polar bears have black skin under their white fur, which helps them absorb heat from the sun.

The London Underground is the oldest subway system in the world.

Answer: Not Bullshit - The London Underground, opened in 1863, is the world's oldest underground railway network.

The Statue of Liberty was originally designed for the Suez Canal in Egypt.

Answer: Not Bullshit - The Statue of Liberty's designer, Frédéric Auguste Bartholdi, initially proposed a similar concept for the Suez Canal, which was not realized.

Bhutan is the only country in the world with a negative carbon footprint.

Answer: Not Bullshit - Bhutan is notable for its extensive forestation, which absorbs more carbon dioxide than the country emits, making its carbon footprint negative.

The Pyramids of Giza are the only remaining Ancient Wonder of the World.

Answer: Not Bullshit - The Great Pyramid of Giza is the only one of the original Seven Wonders of the Ancient World still in existence.

The Bermuda Triangle is recognized by the US Navy as an area of unusual geographic phenomena.

Answer: Bullshit - The US Navy does not recognize the Bermuda Triangle as an area of unusual geographic phenomena or as an official region at all.

The Maldives will disappear under the sea in the next 100 years.

Answer: Bullshit - While the Maldives is one of the world's lowest-lying countries and at high risk from rising sea levels, predictions about its disappearance vary and depend on future sea level rises.

Bonus Fact: A bolt of lightning contains enough energy to toast 100,000 slices of bread.

Health & Wellness

Drinking cold water after meals causes cancer.

Answer: Bullshit - There's no scientific evidence to support the claim that drinking cold water after meals can cause cancer.

Cracking your knuckles leads to arthritis.

Answer: Bullshit - Studies have found no direct correlation between knuckle cracking and the development of arthritis.

Standing too close to a microwave can give you cancer.

Answer: Bullshit - Microwaves are designed to keep radiation inside, and there's no evidence that standing close to a microwave in good condition poses cancer risks.

Detox diets are necessary to remove toxins from the body.

Answer: Bullshit - The liver and kidneys naturally detoxify and remove impurities and toxins from the body. Most detox diets have no scientific basis for their claims.

Eating chocolate causes acne.

Answer: Bullshit - There's no conclusive evidence that chocolate directly causes acne, though diet and sugary foods can affect the skin in some people.

An apple a day keeps the doctor away.

Answer: Bullshit - While eating apples contributes to a healthy diet, it's not a guarantee against medical visits.

Bonus Fact: The inventor of the frisbee, Walter Frederick Morrison, was turned into a frisbee after he died; his ashes were molded into a limited number of frisbees.

You can catch a cold by being out in cold weather.

Answer: Bullshit - Colds are caused by viruses, not cold weather. However, cold weather can indirectly increase the risk by keeping people indoors and in close contact.

Yoga can improve your mental health.

Answer: Not Bullshit - Studies have shown that yoga can reduce stress, anxiety, and depression, improving overall mental health.

Skipping breakfast can cause weight gain.

Answer: Bullshit - Weight gain is more about overall caloric intake and expenditure than specific meal timing. Skipping breakfast does not automatically cause weight gain.

Bonus Fact: Laughter can burn calories! Research suggests that laughing for about 10 to 15 minutes a day can burn approximately 10 to 40 calories. While it won't replace a workout, it does show that humor has some surprising benefits for your body!

Sleeping less than 7 hours a night can shorten your lifespan.

Answer: Not Bullshit - Chronic sleep deprivation has been linked to various health issues, including heart disease and shortened lifespan.

Vaccines can cause autism.

Answer: Bullshit - Extensive research has shown no link between vaccines and autism. This myth has been debunked numerous times.

Sitting too close to the TV damages your eyesight.

Answer: Bullshit - While sitting close to a TV can cause eyestrain, it doesn't cause permanent damage to eyesight.

Eating eggs every day is bad for your heart.

Answer: Bullshit - Recent studies suggest that, for most people, eating eggs in moderation does not significantly impact heart disease risk.

Listening to classical music makes you smarter.

Answer: Bullshit - Known as the "Mozart effect," the claim that listening to classical music can increase intelligence is not supported by scientific evidence.

Spicy food can cause ulcers.

Answer: Bullshit - Most ulcers are caused by H. pylori bacteria or the use of certain medications, not by consuming spicy food.

Regular exercise can reduce the risk of chronic diseases.

Answer: Not Bullshit - Regular physical activity is linked to reduced risks of diseases such as heart disease, diabetes, and cancer.

Reading in dim light ruins your eyesight.

Answer: Bullshit - Reading in dim light can cause eye strain but doesn't cause permanent damage to eyesight.

Coconut oil is a heart-healthy cooking alternative.

Answer: Bullshit - Coconut oil is high in saturated fats, which can raise levels of bad cholesterol and potentially harm heart health.

Using a cellphone at night can disrupt your sleep.

Answer: Not Bullshit - The blue light emitted by screens can interfere with the production of melatonin, a hormone that regulates sleep.

Drinking alcohol warms your body.

Answer: Bullshit - Alcohol may create a temporary feeling of warmth but actually lowers your core body temperature.

Chewing gum stays in your stomach for seven years if swallowed.

Answer: Bullshit - Swallowed gum passes through the digestive system relatively unchanged and is excreted, not retained for years.

Taking vitamin C supplements can prevent the common cold.

Answer: Bullshit - While vitamin C supports the immune system, evidence that it can prevent the common cold is weak.

A gluten-free diet is healthier for everyone.

Answer: Bullshit - A gluten-free diet is essential for those with celiac disease or gluten sensitivity but not necessarily healthier for everyone else.

You can sweat out toxins in a sauna.

Answer: Bullshit - While saunas can be relaxing and beneficial for circulation, the body primarily removes toxins through the liver and kidneys, not sweat.

Artificial sweeteners are healthier than sugar.

Answer: Bullshit - Artificial sweeteners are not necessarily healthier; their effects on weight management and long-term health are still debated.

Eating soy can increase breast cancer risk.

Answer: Bullshit - Most research indicates that soy, in moderation, does not increase the risk of breast cancer and may even offer protective benefits.

Drinking milk increases mucus production.

Answer: Bullshit - No scientific evidence supports the claim that milk increases mucus production in most people.

Flossing is unnecessary if you brush your teeth regularly.

Answer: Bullshit - Flossing removes plaque and food particles between teeth where a toothbrush can't reach, helping to prevent gum disease and cavities.

Bonus Fact: Eating too many carrots can turn your skin orange! This condition, called carotenemia, occurs when there's an excess of beta-carotene in the blood, typically from consuming large amounts of carrots or other beta-carotene-rich foods. While it's generally harmless, it can give your skin an orange hue.

History & World Cultures

The Great Pyramid of Giza was originally white.

Answer: Not Bullshit - The Great Pyramid was originally covered in casing stones made of highly polished Tura limestone, which would have made it gleam in the sun, appearing white.

Napoleon Bonaparte was extremely short.

Answer: Bullshit - Napoleon was of average height for his time. The misconception about his height likely arises from the difference in French and British measuring units.

The city of Rome was founded by twin brothers Romulus and Remus.

Answer: Bullshit - While this is a famous legend, Rome's foundation is a complex historical process involving various groups and not solely based on the myth of Romulus and Remus.

Vikings wore horned helmets into battle.

Answer: Bullshit - There is no evidence that Vikings wore horned helmets in battle. This image is a product of later folklore and artistic interpretation.

The Great Wall of China was built to protect against the Mongol invasions.

Answer: Bullshit - While part of the Great Wall was built during the Ming Dynasty to fend off Mongol incursions, the construction of different sections of the wall began as early as the 7th century BC, long before the Mongol Empire.

The Forbidden City in Beijing has exactly 9,999 rooms.

Answer: Bullshit - The Forbidden City is said to have around 9,000 rooms, but the exact number varies depending on how one counts the rooms.

The Trojan War was a purely mythical event.

Answer: Bullshit(Sort of) - While the Iliad is a mythological text, there is archaeological evidence suggesting that a war or series of wars did occur in the region of Troy, though details are still debated.

Cleopatra was Egyptian.

Answer: Bullshit - Cleopatra was actually of Macedonian Greek origin, belonging to the Ptolemaic dynasty that ruled Egypt after Alexander the Great's death.

Bonus Fact: Octopuses have three hearts: two pump blood to the gills and one pumps it to the rest of the body.

The Spanish Inquisition was primarily aimed at punishing witches.

Answer: Bullshit - The Spanish Inquisition targeted primarily heretics and those accused of Judaizing and later Muslim converts, with witch hunts playing a relatively minor role.

The Iron Maiden was a common medieval torture device.

Answer: Bullshit - The Iron Maiden is likely a mythologized or exaggerated invention of later periods, with little evidence of its use in medieval Europe.

The phrase "Let them eat cake" was said by Marie Antoinette.

Answer: Bullshit - There's no good historical evidence that Marie Antoinette ever uttered this phrase. It is likely apocryphal or misattributed.

The ancient Greeks believed the Earth was the center of the universe.

Answer: Not Bullshit - The geocentric model was indeed the prevailing cosmological system in ancient Greece, with famous proponents like Aristotle and Ptolemy.

The first Thanksgiving in America was a peaceful and friendly event between Pilgrims and Native Americans.

Answer: Bullshit - The narrative of a peaceful and friendly first Thanksgiving is an oversimplification and idealization of what was a complex and often tense relationship between Native Americans and European settlers.

Marco Polo introduced pasta to Italy from China.

Answer: Bullshit - While Marco Polo did write about eating a type of noodle in China, pasta was already known in Europe, especially in Italy, before his travels.

During the Black Death, doctors wore 'beak masks' filled with aromatic items to protect themselves from the plague.

Answer: Not Bullshit - Plague doctors wore these masks with the belief that the plague was spread through bad air and that the aromatics would help

Batman's Bruce Wayne's name was inspired by the famous Scottish King Robert the Bruce.

Answer: Not Bullshit: Batman Creators Bob Kane and Bill Finger took the name Bruce from Robert the Bruce and Wayne from Anthony Wayne, the general who defeated the british in the Battle of Stony Point.

Bonus Fact: Humans and giraffes have the same number of neck vertebrae: seven.

Language & Linguistics

The English word "nightmare" originally referred to a demon that sits on people's chests while they sleep.

Answer: Not Bullshit - The term "nightmare" comes from the Old English "mare," a mythological demon or goblin who torments others with frightening dreams by sitting on their chest.

The Inuit have over 50 words for snow.

Answer: Not Bullshit - The Inuit languages have a rich vocabulary for different types of snow, reflecting the importance of snow in their environment.

"Butterfly" is the same word in every language.

Answer: Bullshit - The word for "butterfly" varies significantly across languages. However, Amazon is pronounced the same in every language, which is why a famous online retailer chose that word for their business.

The longest word in the English language is "pneumonoultramicroscopicsilicovolcanoconiosis."

Answer: Not Bullshit - This word, referring to a lung disease caused by inhaling very fine ash and sand dust, is often cited as the longest word in the English language.

Esperanto is a completely made-up language that has no native speakers.

Answer: Not Bullshit - Esperanto is an artificial language created in the late 19th century to foster international communication. While it has no native speakers from birth, it has a community of fluent speakers worldwide.

Shakespeare invented the name "Jessica."

Answer: Not Bullshit - The name "Jessica" first appears in Shakespeare's play "The Merchant of Venice."

The phrase "It's all Greek to me" originates from Shakespeare's writings.

Answer: Not Bullshit - This phrase, implying that something is difficult to understand, indeed comes from Shakespeare's play "Julius Caesar."

French was the official language of England for over 300 years.

Answer: Not Bullshit - Following the Norman Conquest in 1066, French became the language of the court, administration, and culture in England, lasting for several centuries.

"Rhythm" is the longest English word without a vowel.

Answer: Not Bullshit - "Rhythm" is among the longest common English words that do not contain any of the traditional vowel letters (A, E, I, O, U).

The word "bookkeeper" (and its derivatives) is the only unhyphenated English word with three consecutive double letters.

Answer: Not Bullshit - "Bookkeeper" and its derivatives, like "bookkeeping," uniquely contain three sets of consecutive double letters without needing a hyphen.

"Orange" was the color named after the fruit, not the other way around.

Answer: Not Bullshit - The color orange was named after the fruit, as the word for the fruit came into English from Arabic and Persian sources.

The word "set" has the most definitions in the English language.

Answer: Not Bullshit - The word "set" holds the record for the most definitions in a single word, according to the Oxford English Dictionary.

A "mondegreen" is a term for a misheard lyric in a song.

Answer: Not Bullshit - The term "mondegreen" describes a misheard phrase in a song that gives it a new meaning. Such as "Hold me closer, Tony Danza" instead of "Tiny Dancer"

The dot over the letter "i" and "j" is called a "tittle."

Answer: Not Bullshit - The small dot over "i" and "j" is indeed called a tittle.

"Typewriter" is the longest word that can be typed using only the top row of a QWERTY keyboard.

Answer: Not Bullshit - "Typewriter" can be typed entirely from the top row of letters on a QWERTY keyboard.

"Queue" is the only word in the English language that is still pronounced the same way when the last four letters are removed.

Answer: Not Bullshit - When you remove the last four letters from "queue," you are left with "q," which is pronounced the same.

The word "alphabet" comes from the first two letters of the Greek alphabet: alpha and beta.

Answer: Not Bullshit - The word "alphabet" indeed derives from the first two letters of the Greek alphabet.

Bonus Fact: In the Cambodian language Khmer, the word "mother" has the longest alphabetic spelling in the world: "□□□□," which is transliterated as "m'nhér" and contains only three characters but is written with 74 individual strokes.

"Palindrome" is itself a palindrome.

Answer: Bullshit - A palindrome is a word or phrase that reads the same backward as forward, which "palindrome" does not.

There are no words in the English language that rhyme with "orange," "silver," or "month."

Answer: Bullshit - While these words are notoriously difficult to rhyme, near rhymes exist, and poets often use creative language to work around such challenges. Sporange, Chilver and Oneth are best suited

The Korean alphabet, Hangul, was designed to be so simple that a wise man can learn it in a morning, and a fool can learn it in the space of ten days.

Answer: Not Bullshit - Hangul was created in the 15th century by King Sejong the Great and his scholars to be easy to learn and promote literacy.

"Go!" is the shortest complete sentence in the English language.

Answer: Not Bullshit - "Go!" is a complete sentence with a subject (implied "you") and a verb.

The name "Wendy" was invented by J.M. Barrie for the novel "Peter Pan."

Answer: Not Bullshit - The name "Wendy" became popularized after J.M. Barrie used it in "Peter Pan."

"Unfriend" is a new word that emerged from social media.

Answer: Bullshit - The verb "to unfriend" dates back to the 13th century, though its popularity surged with social media.

The Chinese language has over 50,000 characters.

Answer: Not Bullshit - The Chinese writing system consists of tens of thousands of characters, though a much smaller number is used in daily communication.

"Cwm" (a Welsh word used in English) is the longest English word without a vowel.

Answer: Not Bullshit - "Cwm," a term for a steep-walled semicircular basin in a mountain, sometimes used in English, is one of the longest vowel-less words.

The original Latin alphabet did not contain the letters U, J, and W.

Answer: Not Bullshit - The U and V were once the same letter, as were I and J, and W evolved from VV or UU in various languages.

"I am." is the shortest complete sentence in the English language.

Answer: Bullshit - "Go!" is actually the shortest sentence in the English Languateexample of a short, complete sentence, with a subject and a verb.

The term "laser" is an acronym.

Answer: Not Bullshit - "Laser" stands for "Light Amplification by Stimulated Emission of Radiation."

The Japanese language uses four different writing systems.

Answer: Not Bullshit - Japanese uses kanji, hiragana, katakana, and romaji.

"Xenophobia" is the fear of the letter X.

Answer: Bullshit - Xenophobia refers to the fear or hatred of strangers or foreigners, not the letter X. The fear of the letter X is Xinoaxphobia, although it is not an official medical term.

Bonus Fact: A group of jellyfish is called a smack.

Movies & Entertainment

'Psycho' was the first American film to show a toilet flushing.

Answer: Not Bullshit - Alfred Hitchcock's 'Psycho' was indeed the first American film to show a toilet flushing on screen.

The phrase "Beam me up, Scotty" was never actually said in the original 'Star Trek' series.

Answer: Not Bullshit - The exact phrase "Beam me up, Scotty" was never uttered in the original 'Star Trek' series.

Walt Disney holds the record for the most Academy Awards won by an individual.

Answer: Not Bullshit - Walt Disney won 22 competitive Academy Awards from 59 nominations, holding the record for the most Oscars won by an individual.

A real skeleton was used in the filming of the original 'Poltergeist' movie.

Answer: Not Bullshit - Real skeletons were used during the filming of the swimming pool scene in 'Poltergeist.'

The movie 'Jaws' was filmed in the actual ocean and not in a studio.

Answer: Not Bullshit - Much of 'Jaws' was filmed in the Atlantic Ocean off the coast of Martha's Vineyard, which contributed to the film's authentic and terrifying feel.

'Casablanca' was the first film to win the Academy Award for Best Picture.

Answer: Bullshit - The first film to win the Academy Award for Best Picture was 'Wings' in 1929. 'Casablanca' won Best Picture in 1944.

Bonus Fact: A narwhal's tusk is actually a tooth that can grow up to 10 feet long.

The character Darth Vader says "Luke, I am your father" in 'The Empire Strikes Back.'

Answer: Bullshit - The actual line is "No, I am your father."

The 'Harry Potter' films were all directed by the same person.

Answer: Bullshit - The 'Harry Potter' series had four directors: Chris Columbus, Alfonso Cuarón, Mike Newell, and David Yates.

Marilyn Monroe was the first choice to play the lead in 'Breakfast at Tiffany's.'

Answer: Not Bullshit - Truman Capote, who wrote the novel, originally envisioned Marilyn Monroe for the role of Holly Golightly, but Audrey Hepburn ultimately played the part.

The movie 'Titanic' had a higher production cost than the actual Titanic ship.

Answer: Not Bullshit - Adjusted for inflation, the production cost of the movie 'Titanic' was indeed higher than the cost to build the original ship.

Leonardo DiCaprio's first Oscar win was for 'Titanic.'

Answer: Bullshit - Leonardo DiCaprio's first Oscar win was for Best Actor in 'The Revenant' (2016), not for 'Titanic.'

The first feature-length animated movie was created by Disney.

Answer: Not Bullshit - Disney's 'Snow White and the Seven Dwarfs' (1937) is considered the first feature-length animated film in full color and sound.

Bonus Fact: Bananas glow blue under black lights due to the breakdown of chlorophyll as they ripen.

'The Godfather' movie is a faithful adaptation of the book.

Answer: Not Bullshit - While there are some differences, 'The Godfather' film is largely faithful to Mario Puzo's novel.

Sean Connery wore a toupee in all of his James Bond films.

Answer: Not Bullshit - Sean Connery began losing his hair at a young age and wore a toupee in all of his appearances as James Bond.

The voice of Yoda and Miss Piggy were performed by the same person.

Answer: Not Bullshit - Frank Oz provided the voices for both Yoda in 'Star Wars' and Miss Piggy in 'The Muppets.'

'Gone with the Wind' is the highest-grossing film of all time, adjusted for inflation.

Answer: Not Bullshit - When adjusted for inflation, 'Gone with the Wind' holds the record for the highest-grossing film.

The original cut of 'Blade Runner' included a happy ending against the director's wishes.

Answer: Not Bullshit - The original theatrical release of 'Blade Runner' included a happy ending that was not part of Ridley Scott's original vision.

'Forrest Gump' is based on a true story.

Answer: Bullshit - 'Forrest Gump' is based on a novel by Winston Groom and is a work of fiction, though it references historical events and figures.

All of the clocks in the movie 'Pulp Fiction' are stuck at 4:20.

Answer: Bullshit - Not all clocks in 'Pulp Fiction' are set to 4:20, though this rumor has circulated as part of the film's lore.

Bonus Fact: Some species of bamboo can grow up to 35 inches in a single day.

The film 'Amadeus' is a historically accurate portrayal of Mozart's life.

Answer: Bullshit - While based on historical figures, 'Amadeus' takes significant artistic liberties with the lives and relationship of Mozart and Salieri.

'The Silence of the Lambs' was the first horror film to win an Academy Award for Best Picture.

Answer: Not Bullshit - 'The Silence of the Lambs' is considered by many to be a horror film, and it won the Academy Award for Best Picture in 1992.

Audrey Hepburn sang all her songs in 'My Fair Lady.'

Answer: Bullshit - While Audrey Hepburn did record the songs, most of her singing was dubbed by Marni Nixon.

'Raiders of the Lost Ark' was the first Indiana Jones movie.

Answer: Not Bullshit - 'Raiders of the Lost Ark' (1981) is the first film in the Indiana Jones series.

The film '2001: A Space Odyssey' includes dialogue in its first and last 30 minutes.

Answer: Bullshit - '2001: A Space Odyssey' is known for its long sequences without dialogue, including its opening and closing scenes.

'Schindler's List' was originally released in color and later changed to black and white.

Answer: Bullshit - 'Schindler's List' was intentionally shot in black and white to reflect its historical period, except for a few selective color scenes.

Bonus Fact: Alaska is the only state whose name can be typed on one row of a standard keyboard.

**'Home Alone' was directed by Steven
Spielberg.**

Answer: Bullshit - 'Home Alone' was directed
by Chris Columbus, though Steven Spielberg
was a prominent filmmaker of the era.

**Bonus Fact: In the movie The Wizard of Oz
(1939), the snow used in the poppy field scene
was actually asbestos, a substance that we
now know is highly toxic. At the time, it was
commonly used for fake snow in films.**

Music & Celebrities

Elvis Presley was a natural blonde.

Answer: Not Bullshit - Elvis Presley was naturally blond but started dyeing his hair black for an edgier look early in his career.

The Beatles originally started as a skiffle band named The Quarrymen.

Answer: Not Bullshit - Before they became The Beatles, the band indeed started as a skiffle group named The Quarrymen.

Mozart and Beethoven were contemporaries who frequently collaborated.

Answer: Bullshit - While Mozart and Beethoven were alive during overlapping times, there's no evidence they ever met or collaborated.

Beyoncé has won more Grammy Awards than any other female artist.

Answer: Not Bullshit - As of this publication, Beyoncé holds the record for the most Grammy Awards won by a female artist.

Jimi Hendrix couldn't read music.

Answer: Not Bullshit - Jimi Hendrix was largely self-taught and did not read music, yet he became one of the most influential guitarists in history.

Keanu Reeves performed all his own stunts in the 'John Wick' series.

Answer: Bullshit - While Keanu Reeves performed many of his own stunts, professional stunt performers were also involved in the series.

Freddie Mercury had a four-octave vocal range.

Answer: Not Bullshit - Freddie Mercury was renowned for his powerful voice and extensive vocal range, which was close to four octaves.

Taylor Swift started her music career in rock music before switching to country and pop.

Answer: Bullshit - Taylor Swift started her career in country music before transitioning to pop and alternative.

Michael Jackson patented a pair of anti-gravity shoes.

Answer: Not Bullshit - Michael Jackson co-held a patent for a shoe design that allowed the illusion of defying gravity, used in performances like "Smooth Criminal."

Prince played every instrument on his debut album, 'For You.'

Answer: Not Bullshit - Prince played all 27 instruments on his debut album, showcasing his multi-instrumental talents.

Adele was discovered on MySpace.

Answer: Not Bullshit - Adele's music caught the attention of XL Recordings after a friend posted her demo on MySpace.

Leonardo DiCaprio's first Oscar win was for 'The Wolf of Wall Street.'

Answer: Bullshit - Leonardo DiCaprio's first Oscar win was for Best Actor in 'The Revenant' (2016), not 'The Wolf of Wall Street.'

Madonna has a degree in physics.

Answer: Bullshit - Madonna does not have a degree in physics. She attended the University of Michigan on a dance scholarship before dropping out to pursue her music career.

Lady Gaga's real name is Stefani Joanne Angelina Germanotta.

Answer: Not Bullshit - Stefani Joanne Angelina Germanotta is indeed Lady Gaga's real name.

Bob Marley was buried with a soccer ball, his guitar, and a bud of marijuana.

Answer: Not Bullshit - Bob Marley was buried with his guitar, a soccer ball, a Bible, and marijuana.

Katy Perry began her music career as a gospel singer.

Answer: Not Bullshit - Katy Perry released a gospel album under her birth name, Katy Hudson, before switching to pop music.

Meryl Streep has been nominated for an Academy Award more times than any other actor or actress.

Answer: Not Bullshit - Meryl Streep holds the record for the most Academy Award nominations for any actor.

David Bowie invented the internet.

Answer: Bullshit - While David Bowie was an early adopter of the internet and had innovative ideas about its use in music and art, he did not invent the internet.

Rihanna's hit "Umbrella" was originally written for Britney Spears.

Answer: Not Bullshit - "Umbrella" was indeed offered to Britney Spears first, but her label rejected it, and Rihanna went on to record the song.

Bonus Fact: There are more stars in the universe than grains of sand on all the world's beaches.

Johnny Cash's "Ring of Fire" was actually written about a spicy food experience.

Answer: Bullshit - "Ring of Fire" was co-written by June Carter Cash and Merle Kilgore and is about falling in love, not about spicy food.

Jennifer Lawrence was discovered while on vacation in New York.

Answer: Not Bullshit - Jennifer Lawrence was spotted by a talent scout while visiting New York City with her family.

The Rolling Stones were named after a song by Muddy Waters.

Answer: Not Bullshit - The band took its name from Muddy Waters' song "Rollin' Stone."

Bonus Fact: A jiffy is an actual unit of time: 1/100th of a second.

Bruce Springsteen's "Born in the USA" is a patriotic anthem celebrating American pride.

Answer: Bullshit - Despite its anthemic chorus, "Born in the USA" is a critique of the treatment of Vietnam veterans and the American dream.

Whitney Houston holds the record for the most consecutive number-one hits on the Billboard Hot 100.

Answer: Not Bullshit - Whitney Houston set a record with seven consecutive number-one singles on the Billboard Hot 100.

Elton John was knighted by Queen Elizabeth for his contributions to music and charitable work.

Answer: Not Bullshit - Sir Elton John was knighted in 1998 for his services to music and charitable causes.

The original name of the band Queen was "The Royal Family."

Answer: Bullshit - The band was not originally called "The Royal Family"; they chose the name "Queen" for its universal appeal and imagery.

Dolly Parton once entered a Dolly Parton look-alike contest and lost.

Answer: Not Bullshit - Dolly Parton has humorously recounted entering a look-alike contest and not winning, as the judges did not recognize her.

Frank Sinatra was offered the leading role in 'The Godfather' but turned it down.

Answer: Bullshit - While Sinatra was rumored to be interested in the role of Vito Corleone, the role was never officially offered to him. Marlon Brando was cast instead.

Bonus Fact: Mozart once composed a piece titled "A Musical Joke" that includes intentional mistakes, such as awkward key changes and clashing harmonies, meant to poke fun at lesser-skilled composers of his time.

Amy Winehouse's "Back to Black" album was recorded in just two weeks.

Answer: Not Bullshit - Amy Winehouse's critically acclaimed album 'Back to Black' was indeed recorded in a very short period, though some pre-production and writing took place earlier.

Charlie Chaplin once entered a Charlie Chaplin look-alike contest and came in third.

Answer: Not Bullshit - This popular story has been circulated about Chaplin, though details vary and its complete accuracy is debated.

Bonus Fact: In 2007, Prince performed at the Super Bowl halftime show in pouring rain, making it the first and only time it has rained during a Super Bowl halftime performance. Despite the slippery stage and electrical hazards, Prince played an iconic rendition of "Purple Rain" with no issues, solidifying his performance as one of the greatest in Super Bowl history.

Politics & Law

The United States Constitution was the first written constitution in the world.

Answer: Bullshit - While the U.S. Constitution is one of the oldest functioning written constitutions, it was not the first. The Constitution of San Marino, dating back to 1600, is among the earliest.

A filibuster can last indefinitely in the U.S. Senate.

Answer: Bullshit - While filibusters can significantly delay legislative action, rules such as the cloture rule (requiring 60 votes) can end a filibuster.

Bonus Fact: The first oranges weren't orange; they were green. Oranges in warmer regions, like Vietnam and Thailand, stay green throughout their lifetime.

In the United Kingdom, the Prime Minister can dissolve Parliament at any time.

Answer: Bullshit - The Fixed-term Parliaments Act of 2011 limits the circumstances under which the Prime Minister can dissolve Parliament, requiring a two-thirds majority in the House of Commons or a vote of no confidence that is not followed by a vote of confidence within 14 days.

The President of Switzerland serves for life.

Answer: Bullshit - Switzerland has a Federal Council, and the presidency rotates among its members annually.

Vatican City is the only country in the world that is unable to host embassies.

Answer: Bullshit - Embassies to the Holy See (Vatican City) are located in Rome, Italy, due to the city-state's small size, not because it's unable to host them.

**The concept of "innocent until proven guilty"
originated in Roman law.**

Answer: Not Bullshit - This principle has its
roots in Roman legal principles and has been a
cornerstone of legal systems influenced by
Roman law.

**New Zealand was the first country to grant
women the right to vote.**

Answer: Not Bullshit - New Zealand granted
women the right to vote in 1893, making it the
first self-governing country to do so.

**The International Criminal Court has the
authority to prosecute individuals for crimes
committed in any country.**

Answer: Bullshit - The ICC can only prosecute
individuals for crimes committed in member
states or if the case is referred to the ICC by the
United Nations Security Council.

"Gerrymandering" is named after a former U.S. President.

Answer: Bullshit - Gerrymandering is named after Elbridge Gerry, a governor of Massachusetts, not a president, who in 1812 signed a bill that created a contorted-shaped electoral district.

In France, it's illegal to name a pig "Napoleon."

Answer: Bullshit - There's no such specific law in France. This myth is popularized by George Orwell's "Animal Farm," where such a rule is part of the story.

The World Bank can grant loans to individuals.

Answer: Bullshit - The World Bank grants loans primarily to countries for development projects, not to individuals.

The United Nations has a standing army.

Answer: Bullshit - The UN doesn't have its own standing army but relies on troops contributed by member states for peacekeeping missions.

Women were allowed to vote in ancient Athens.

Answer: Bullshit - In ancient Athens, only male citizens had the right to vote. Women, slaves, and foreigners were excluded from the democratic process.

The Magna Carta was the first document to limit the power of the king in England.

Answer: Not Bullshit - Signed in 1215, the Magna Carta is considered one of the first legal documents to limit the powers of the English monarch.

In the United States, the Supreme Court justices are elected by the public.

Answer: Bullshit - Supreme Court justices are nominated by the President and must be confirmed by the Senate.

"Lobbying" derives from the practice of influencing legislators in the lobby of a legislative building.

Answer: Not Bullshit - The term does originate from the practice of advocates waiting in the lobbies of legislative buildings to speak to lawmakers.

Singapore has a law against chewing gum.

Answer: Not Bullshit - Singapore banned the import and sale of chewing gum in 1992, with exceptions made for therapeutic purposes.

Piracy off the coast of Somalia is governed by ancient maritime laws.

Answer: Bullshit - Modern piracy off the coast of Somalia is more a result of lawlessness and economic desperation than any ancient maritime laws.

The African Union has a court with jurisdiction similar to the International Criminal Court.

Answer: Not Bullshit - The African Union supports the African Court on Human and Peoples' Rights, which complements and reinforces the functions of the African Commission on Human and Peoples' Rights.

Switzerland has mandatory military service for all citizens.

Answer: Not Bullshit - Switzerland requires military service for all male citizens, with alternative service options for those who cannot serve for various reasons.

Julius Caesar was the first Roman Emperor.

Answer: Bullshit - While Caesar was a Roman dictator, the first official Roman Emperor was Augustus, Caesar's adopted heir.

The Peace of Westphalia created the modern state system.

Answer: Not Bullshit - The Peace of Westphalia treaties, signed in 1648, are credited with establishing the principles of sovereign states and non-interference, fundamental to the modern international state system.

An absolute monarchy is a government where the king or queen has no real power and serves only as a ceremonial figurehead.

Answer: Bullshit - An absolute monarchy is one where the monarch has almost complete power, as opposed to a constitutional monarchy, where the monarch's powers are limited or ceremonial.

The first female head of government was in the 20th century.

Answer: Not Bullshit - Sirimavo Bandaranaike of Ceylon (now Sri Lanka) became the world's first female prime minister in 1960.

The Socratic method was named after an ancient Greek actor.

Answer: Bullshit - The Socratic method is named after the Greek philosopher Socrates, known for his technique of asking probing questions to stimulate critical thinking and to illuminate ideas.

North Korea and South Korea are still technically at war.

Answer: Not Bullshit - The Korean War ended with an armistice in 1953, not a peace treaty, leaving the two Koreas technically still at war.

Bonus Fact: Bananas glow blue under black lights due to the breakdown of chlorophyll as they ripen.

The European Union has its own army.

Answer: Bullshit - The EU does not have its own standing army but has various security and defense policies and can deploy peacekeeping missions.

The right to bear arms is a universally guaranteed human right.

Answer: Bullshit - The right to bear arms is not universally recognized as a human right; it varies significantly by country and is particularly emphasized in the United States.

Nelson Mandela was the first black president of South Africa.

Answer: Not Bullshit - Nelson Mandela was indeed the first black president of South Africa, elected in 1994 after the end of apartheid.

Bonus Fact: In 1935, the town of Brainerd, Minnesota, elected a man named "Mr. Bones" as mayor. Mr. Bones was a bull terrier who served a full term as mayor after his owner entered him as a joke candidate. His election and service were largely symbolic, and the town council handled all actual governance.

The "Iron Curtain" was a physical barrier that divided Europe during the Cold War.

Answer: Bullshit - The "Iron Curtain" was a metaphorical term used by Winston Churchill to describe the political and ideological division between Western democracies and Eastern communist countries during the Cold War, not a physical barrier.

Science & Nature

Water has a memory and can retain 'information' from substances that were once dissolved in it.

Answer: Bullshit - The claim that water has memory is not supported by scientific evidence and contradicts basic principles of chemistry and physics.

A group of crows is called a 'murder'.

Answer: Not Bullshit - A group of crows is indeed referred to as a 'murder', a term that dates back to at least the 15th century.

Sharks are immune to all known diseases.

Answer: Bullshit - While sharks have a strong immune system, they are not immune to all diseases and can suffer from various ailments, including cancer.

Lightning never strikes in the same place twice.

Answer: Bullshit - Lightning can and often does strike the same place multiple times, especially if it's a tall, isolated object such as the Empire State Building which is struck 25 times per year on average.

Bananas grow on trees.

Answer: Bullshit - Although it appears tree-like, the banana 'tree' is actually a large herbaceous plant. The banana 'trunk' is made of tightly packed leaf bases.

A penny dropped from the top of the Empire State Building could kill someone.

Answer: Bullshit - Due to air resistance, a penny dropped from such a height would not gather enough speed to cause fatal injury.

Humans can distinguish over a million different colors.

Answer: Not Bullshit - Humans can distinguish about 1 million different colors, though this number can vary among individuals.

We only use 10% of our brains.

Answer: Bullshit - Neuroimaging research has shown that we use much more than 10% of our brains, even during simple tasks.

The Great Wall of China is visible from the moon.

Answer: Bullshit - The Great Wall of China is not visible from the moon with the naked eye. This is a common misconception.

Ostriches bury their heads in the sand when scared.

Answer: Bullshit - Ostriches do not actually bury their heads in the sand. This myth likely arose from their behavior of lying low and pressing their necks to the ground when threatened.

A blue whale's heart is as large as a small car.

Answer: Not Bullshit - The heart of a blue whale can be as large as a small car, weighing around 400 pounds and about the size of a small piano.

The sun is yellow.

Answer: Bullshit - The sun is actually all colors mixed together, which appear to us as white light. The sun can appear yellow due to the Earth's atmosphere.

The Sahara Desert is the largest desert in the world.

Answer: Bullshit - The largest desert in the world is Antarctica. Deserts are defined by dryness, not heat, and Antarctica is the driest place on Earth.

Bats are blind.

Answer: Bullshit - Bats are not blind and can see quite well. They use echolocation to navigate in the dark, but their eyes are fully functional.

A bolt of lightning is hotter than the surface of the sun.

Answer: Not Bullshit - The temperature of a lightning bolt can reach approximately 30,000 Kelvin, hotter than the surface of the sun, which is about 5,500 Kelvin.

Humans and dinosaurs coexisted at some point in history.

Answer: Bullshit - Humans and dinosaurs did not coexist. The last dinosaurs died out about 65 million years before humans appeared.

The rings of Saturn are solid.

Answer: Bullshit - Saturn's rings are not solid; they are made up of billions of small ice and rock particles.

A cockroach can live several weeks without its head.

Answer: Not Bullshit - A cockroach can live for several weeks without its head, eventually dying from starvation.

Bonus Fact: The word "nerd" was first coined by Dr. Seuss in his book "If I Ran the Zoo" in 1950.

Mount Everest is the closest point to the sun on Earth.

Answer: Bullshit - Mount Everest is the Earth's highest point above sea level, but the closest point to the sun is actually the summit of Mount Chimborazo in Ecuador, due to the equatorial bulge.

The Amazon Rainforest produces 20% of the world's oxygen.

Answer: Bullshit - This is a common misconception. The Amazon contributes to oxygen production, but the majority of Earth's oxygen comes from the oceans, particularly from phytoplankton.

Venus is the hottest planet in our solar system.

Answer: Not Bullshit - Despite being second from the sun, Venus is the hottest planet due to its thick atmosphere, which traps heat in a runaway greenhouse effect.

The tongue has different zones for each taste.

Answer: Bullshit - The idea that different parts of the tongue are responsible for different tastes is a misconception. All tastes can be detected on all parts of the tongue.

An adult human has fewer bones than a baby.

Answer: Not Bullshit - Babies are born with about 300 bones, but some fuse together as they grow, leaving the average adult with 206 bones.

Chameleons change color to blend into their environment.

Answer: Bullshit - Chameleons change color primarily in response to temperature, mood, and communication with other chameleons, not primarily for camouflage.

Bonus Fact: Koalas sleep up to 22 hours a day. They have one of the lowest energy diets of any mammal.

A full moon affects human behavior.

Answer: Bullshit - Despite popular belief, scientific studies have found no consistent evidence of the moon's phases affecting human behavior.

Water spirals in different directions when draining in different hemispheres.

Answer: Bullshit - The Coriolis effect does not affect water spiraling in sinks or toilets. The direction of water drainage is determined by the shape of the basin and the water's momentum.

Camels store water in their humps.

Answer: Bullshit - Camel humps do not store water. They store fat, which can be converted into water and energy when needed.

The Five-Second Rule for dropped food is scientifically supported.

Answer: Bullshit - The Five-Second Rule, which suggests food is safe to eat if picked up within five seconds of being dropped, is not scientifically valid. Bacteria can attach to food instantly.

Humans can't breathe and swallow at the same time.

Answer: Not Bullshit - Due to the design of the human pharynx, breathing and swallowing cannot occur simultaneously. This is different in newborns, who can breathe and swallow at the same time.

Bonus Fact: The wood frog can hold its pee for up to eight months to survive in the winter.

Sports & Games

Cleveland Indians pitcher Ray Caldwell was struck by lightning while playing for the Cleveland Indians against the Philadelphia Athletics in 1919; despite being knocked unconscious, he refused to leave the game, having pitched 8 2/3 innings, and went on to record the final out for the win.

Answer: Not Bullshit

Basketball was originally played with a soccer ball.

Answer: Not Bullshit - Basketball was initially played with a soccer ball when it was invented in 1891 by James Naismith.

Golf was invented in Scotland.

Answer: Not Bullshit - The modern game of golf originated in 15th-century Scotland, though similar games have been recorded in earlier history.

The Olympic Games were invented by the Romans.

Answer: Bullshit - The Olympic Games originated in ancient Greece, not Rome. The first recorded Olympic Games took place in 776 BC.

Chess was invented in India.

Answer: Not Bullshit - Chess originated in India during the Gupta Empire around the 6th century AD, initially called "Chaturanga."

Polo is the oldest known team sport.

Answer: Not Bullshit - Polo is one of the oldest known team sports, with origins dating back over 2,000 years in ancient Persia.

Soccer balls were originally made from animal bladders.

Answer: Not Bullshit - Early soccer balls were indeed made from inflated animal bladders, specifically pig bladders, before being encased in leather.

Baseball was invented by Abner Doubleday in Cooperstown, New York.

Answer: Bullshit - The myth that Abner Doubleday invented baseball in 1839 has been widely debunked. The game evolved from older bat-and-ball games.

The Tour de France has always been a purely French event.

Answer: Bullshit - Although the Tour de France is a French event, it has included routes passing through neighboring countries and has international participants.

The first Paralympic Games were held in Rome in 1960.

Answer: Not Bullshit - The first official Paralympic Games were indeed held in Rome in 1960, following the 1960 Summer Olympics.

Ping pong was originally played with champagne corks as balls.

Answer: Not Bullshit - Ping pong started as a parlor game in the 19th century, where players initially used books for bats and a champagne cork as the ball.

Michael Phelps has won more Olympic medals than any other athlete in history.

Answer: Not Bullshit - As of my last update, Michael Phelps holds the record for the most Olympic medals won by any athlete.

In tennis, 'Love' means zero or no score.

Answer: Not Bullshit - In tennis, the term 'love' is used to indicate a score of zero.

Bonus Fact: The longest time between two twins being born is 87 days.

FIFA World Cup soccer balls are always made in the host country.

Answer: Bullshit - FIFA World Cup soccer balls are not necessarily made in the host country; they are often manufactured in different countries, including Pakistan and China.

The New York Marathon is the oldest marathon in the world.

Answer: Bullshit - The Boston Marathon, started in 1897, is the oldest annual marathon, predating the New York Marathon.

The huddle in American football was invented by a deaf college.

Answer: Not Bullshit - The huddle in American football was indeed first used by Gallaudet University, a deaf college, to prevent other teams from seeing their sign language.

A 'Perfect Game' in baseball is when a team scores the maximum runs possible.

Answer: Bullshit - A 'Perfect Game' in baseball is when a pitcher does not allow any opposing player to reach base during the entire game.

In the original rules of basketball, dribbling was not allowed.

Answer: Not Bullshit - When basketball was first invented, players could only pass the ball without dribbling.

All professional darts players must stand exactly 7 feet 9.25 inches from the dartboard.

Answer: Not Bullshit - The standard throwing distance in darts is indeed 7 feet 9.25 inches from the dartboard.

Bonus Fact: The fastest goal in soccer history was scored just 2.1 seconds after kickoff by Nawaf Al-Abed of Saudi Arabia's Al-Hilal team during a Prince Faisal bin Fahad Cup game in 2009.

**The modern game of badminton comes from
a game called 'Poona' in India.**

Answer: Not Bullshit - The game of badminton
was developed in British India from the earlier
game called 'Poona.'

**The first Super Bowl was held after the AFL-
NFL merger.**

Answer: Bullshit - The first Super Bowl was
played in 1967, prior to the AFL-NFL merger,
which happened in 1970.

Table tennis is the national sport of China.

Answer: Not Bullshit - Table tennis is
considered the national sport of China, where
it enjoys immense popularity.

In professional boxing, biting is allowed.

Answer: Bullshit - Biting is not allowed in
professional boxing and is considered a serious
foul.

A standard soccer field is larger than an American football field.

Answer: Not Bullshit - A standard soccer field is generally larger than an American football field, with a length up to 120 yards compared to 100 yards.

In cricket, the term 'Duck' is used when a player is out without scoring any runs.

Answer: Not Bullshit - A 'Duck' in cricket refers to a batsman getting out without scoring any runs.

The Olympic gold medal is made entirely of gold.

Answer: Bullshit - Modern Olympic gold medals are primarily made of silver, coated with a thin layer of gold.

Rugby is named after a school in England.

Answer: Not Bullshit - Rugby is named after Rugby School in England, where it is believed the game was first played.

The highest score possible in a single frame of bowling is 30.

Answer: Not Bullshit - In bowling, the highest score in a single frame is 30, achieved by bowling three consecutive strikes.

In golf, a 'Birdie' is one stroke above par.

Answer: Bullshit - A 'Birdie' in golf is one stroke under par, not above.

Bonus Fact: The fastest goal in soccer history was scored just 2.1 seconds after kickoff by Nawaf Al-Abed of Saudi Arabia's Al-Hilal team during a Prince Faisal bin Fahad Cup game in 2009.

Marathon races were originally 26 miles long.

Answer: Bullshit - The original marathon distance varied but became standardized at 26.2 miles (42.195 kilometers) in the 20th century.

Bonus Fact: On June 4, 1974, the Cleveland Indians held a "Ten Cent Beer Night" promotion during a game against the Texas Rangers. The promotion offered beer for just ten cents, leading to excessive drinking among the fans. As the game progressed, the crowd became increasingly unruly and intoxicated. By the ninth inning, the situation had escalated into a full-scale riot, with fans storming the field, throwing objects, and engaging in violent behavior. The umpires had no choice but to forfeit the game to the Texas Rangers due to the chaotic and unsafe conditions.

Technology & Innovation

The QWERTY keyboard layout was designed to slow down typing.

Answer: Not Bullshit - The QWERTY layout was designed in the 19th century to prevent typewriter keys from jamming, not necessarily to slow typing but to separate commonly used letter pairs.

Turning off your computer every night is bad for it.

Answer: Bullshit - Regularly turning off your computer can actually be beneficial, as it can help with software updates and prevent long-term wear from overheating.

The first computer virus was created in the early 2000s.

Answer: Bullshit - The first known computer virus, called "Creeper," was detected in the early 1970s on ARPANET, the precursor to the internet.

Bluetooth technology is named after a 10th-century king.

Answer: Not Bullshit - Bluetooth technology is indeed named after Harald "Bluetooth" Gormsson, a king who united Denmark and Norway, as the technology unites communication protocols.

The Great Wall of China can be seen from space with the naked eye.

Answer: Bullshit - Contrary to popular belief, the Great Wall of China is not visible from space with the naked eye.

Eating while using a computer can damage its internal components.

Answer: Not Bullshit - Crumbs and liquids from eating around a computer can cause damage if they get inside the machine.

LED bulbs are harmful to your health.

Answer: Bullshit - LED bulbs are not inherently harmful to health; they are energy-efficient and have a lower risk of burning out compared to traditional bulbs.

Solar panels do not work on cloudy days.

Answer: Bullshit - Solar panels can still generate power on cloudy days, although their efficiency is reduced compared to sunny days.

The internet weighs about the same as a strawberry.

Answer: Not Bullshit - When considering the electronic data stored in all the internet's servers, the weight, calculated from the electrons in the data, is estimated to be around 50 grams, approximately the weight of a strawberry.

Using a mobile phone at a gas station can cause an explosion.

Answer: Bullshit - There is no evidence that using a mobile phone at a gas station can cause an explosion. The warning is a precaution against potential static electricity.

Artificial Intelligence can function exactly like the human brain.

Answer: Bullshit - While AI can mimic some aspects of human cognition, it does not function exactly like the human brain, which is far more complex and nuanced.

You should drain your smartphone battery completely before recharging.

Answer: Bullshit - Modern lithium-ion batteries perform better when not fully drained. Partial discharges and charges are preferable.

3D printers can only use plastic as a printing material.

Answer: Bullshit - 3D printers can use a variety of materials, including metal, resin, and even living cells.

The 'cloud' in cloud computing is a physical cloud.

Answer: Bullshit - The 'cloud' refers to servers accessed over the internet and the software and databases that run on those servers, not a physical cloud.

Email is older than the World Wide Web.

Answer: Not Bullshit - Email was developed in the 1970s, while the World Wide Web was invented in 1989.

Bonus Fact: In 2014, a man named Patrick McConlogue offered a homeless man named Leo Grand a choice: $100 in cash or the opportunity to learn how to code. Leo chose to learn coding, and within a few months, he developed and launched his own app called "Trees for Cars," aimed at reducing carbon footprints through carpooling.

Wi-Fi radiation can cause cancer.

Answer: Bullshit - There is no conclusive evidence that Wi-Fi radiation poses a cancer risk to humans. Wi-Fi emits low-level non-ionizing radiation, which is not harmful like ionizing radiation.

Self-driving cars are completely accident-proof.

Answer: Bullshit - While self-driving cars can reduce the risk of accidents, they are not completely accident-proof and can still encounter unpredictable situations.

Virtual Reality can cause permanent eye damage.

Answer: Bullshit - While prolonged use can cause eye strain or discomfort, there's no evidence that virtual reality causes permanent eye damage.

The 'Dark Web' is entirely illegal.

Answer: Bullshit - The Dark Web is a part of the internet that is not indexed by search engines, and while it can be used for illegal activities, not everything on it is unlawful.

Space travel can reverse aging.

Answer: Bullshit - Space travel does not reverse aging. Astronauts in space can experience changes due to microgravity, but these are not related to the fundamental process of aging.

Voice recognition technology was initially developed for military use.

Answer: Not Bullshit - Early development of voice recognition technology was indeed funded and used by the military.

Random Facts

Bananas are berries, but strawberries aren't.

Answer: Not Bullshit - According to botanical definitions, bananas qualify as berries, while strawberries do not.

Honey never spoils.

Answer: Not Bullshit - Archaeologists have found pots of honey in ancient Egyptian tombs that are over 3,000 years old and still edible.

A day on Venus is longer than a year on Venus.

Answer: Not Bullshit - Venus takes 243 Earth days to rotate once but only 225 Earth days to orbit the Sun.

There are more stars in the universe than grains of sand on Earth.

Answer: Not Bullshit - The observable universe contains approximately 1,000,000,000,000,000,000,000,000 stars.

A single strand of spaghetti is called a "spaghetto."

Answer: Not Bullshit - The Italian language has singular forms for its food names.

Cows have best friends.

Answer: Not Bullshit - Studies have shown that cows form close bonds and can become stressed when separated from their friends.

Octopuses have three hearts.

Answer: Not Bullshit - Two pump blood to the gills, while one pumps it to the rest of the body.

There is a species of jellyfish that is immortal.

Answer: Not Bullshit - Turritopsis dohrnii can revert back to its juvenile form after reaching maturity, effectively making it immortal.

Wombat poop is cube-shaped.

Answer: Not Bullshit - This unique shape prevents it from rolling away and marks territory.

An eagle can kill a young deer and fly away with it.

Answer: Not Bullshit - The golden eagle has been known to prey on deer, swooping down and lifting them off the ground.

You can hear a blue whale's heartbeat from more than 2 miles away.

Answer: Not Bullshit - Their hearts can weigh as much as a small car and beat loudly enough to be heard from a great distance.

Tigers have striped skin, not just striped fur.

Answer: Not Bullshit - The pattern is part of their skin pigmentation.

Scotland's national animal is the unicorn.

Answer: Not Bullshit - Chosen for its association with purity and power in Celtic mythology.

A shrimp's heart is in its head.

Answer: Not Bullshit - Specifically, it's located in the thorax, which is just behind the head.

There are more fake flamingos in the world than real ones.

Answer: Not Bullshit - The plastic lawn flamingos outnumber real flamingos.

A bolt of lightning contains enough energy to toast 100,000 slices of bread.

Answer: Not Bullshit - That's about 5 billion joules of energy.

There are more possible iterations of a game of chess than there are atoms in the known universe.

Answer: Not Bullshit - The number of unique chess games is astronomically high.

The inventor of the Pringles can is now buried in one.

Answer: Not Bullshit - Fred Baur requested to be buried in one of his iconic cans.

A day on Mercury is twice as long as a year on Mercury.

Answer: Not Bullshit - It takes 176 Earth days for Mercury to rotate once but only 88 Earth days to orbit the Sun.

An apple, potato, and onion all taste the same if you eat them with your nose plugged.

Answer: Not Bullshit - Your sense of smell plays a huge role in your sense of taste, and without it, these foods are nearly indistinguishable.

The popular children's book series and subsequent animated series based on cute anthropomorphic bears who learn moral and safety lessons in each episode and book is called the "Berenstein Bears."

Answer: Bullshit - Many people remember it as "Berenstein Bears," but it is actually "Berenstain Bears."

The animated television series featuring iconic cartoon characters like Bugs Bunny and Daffy Duck is spelled "Looney Toons."

Answer: Bullshit - Some remember it as "Looney Toons," but the correct spelling is "Looney Tunes."

The Monopoly Man, also known as Rich
Uncle Pennybags, is depicted with a monocle.

Answer: Bullshit - Many recall the Monopoly
Man having a monocle, but he does not.

The popular Pokémon character Pikachu is
often depicted with a black tip at the end of
its tail.

Answer: Bullshit - Some people remember
Pikachu's tail having a black tip, but it is all
yellow.

The logo for the Fruit of the Loom brand
includes a cornucopia behind the fruits.

Answer: Bullshit - Many believe the logo
includes a cornucopia, but it does not.

The famous line from Snow White and the
Seven Dwarfs is "Mirror, mirror on the wall,
who is the fairest of them all?"

Answer: Bullshit - The line from Snow White is
actually "Magic mirror on the wall."

The iconic line from Star Wars: The Empire Strikes Back is "Luke, I am your father."

Answer: Bullshit - The famous line from Star Wars is actually "No, I am your father."

The Queen song "We Are the Champions" ends with the lyrics "of the world" in the studio recording.

Answer: Bullshit - Many remember the Queen song ending with "of the world," but it doesn't in the studio version.

The chocolate candy bar brand "KitKat" includes a hyphen in its name, making it "Kit-Kat."

Answer: Bullshit - Some people recall there being a hyphen between "Kit" and "Kat" (Kit-Kat), but there isn't.

The children's book character Curious George is depicted with a tail.

Answer: Bullshit - Many remember Curious George having a tail, but he never had one.

The air freshener brand is spelled "Febreeze."

Answer: Bullshit - Many think it's spelled "Febreeze," but the correct spelling is "Febreze."

The brand of hot dogs and lunch meats is spelled "Oscar Meyer."

Answer: Bullshit - Some remember it being spelled "Oscar Meyer," but it's "Oscar Mayer."

The popular television series about four women living in New York City is called "Sex in the City."

Answer: Bullshit - Many people remember the TV show as "Sex in the City," but it is "Sex and the City."

The animated television show about a prehistoric family is called "The Flinstones."

Answer: Bullshit - Some recall it as "The Flinstones," but the correct name is "The Flintstones."

The color chartreuse is a shade of pink.

Answer: Bullshit - Some people think the color chartreuse is a shade of pink, but it is actually a shade of green.

The opening line of Mr. Rogers' theme song is "It's a beautiful day in the neighborhood."

Answer: Bullshit - The opening line is often remembered as "It's a beautiful day in the neighborhood," but it is "It's a beautiful day in this neighborhood."

The Star Wars character C-3PO is entirely gold.

Answer: Bullshit - Many remember C-3PO as being entirely gold, but he has a silver leg in the original trilogy.

The line from Forrest Gump is "Life is like a box of chocolates."

Answer: Bullshit - The line from Forrest Gump is actually "Life was like a box of chocolates."

The movie about a vampire interview is titled "Interview with a Vampire."

Answer: Bullshit - The movie is often remembered as "Interview with a Vampire," but it is actually "Interview with the Vampire."

Al Capone played a significant role in the implementation of milk expiration dates after his niece became seriously ill from drinking spoiled milk

Answer: Not Bullsh*t - Capone's efforts did lead to the widespread adoption of milk expiration dates, which remain a standard practice today.

High heels were originally for men and were first worn by Persian men in the 10th century to help secure their feet in stirrups. They became fashionable for European men in the 17th century before transitioning to women's fashion.

Answer: Not Bullshit - High heels were indeed first worn by men for practical purposes and later became a fashion statement in Europe.

In 18th-century Europe, tomatoes were nicknamed "poison apples" because aristocrats would often get sick and die after eating them. The real culprit was the lead in their pewter plates, which reacted with the tomatoes' acidity.

Answer: Not Bullshit - Tomatoes were once considered poisonous due to the reaction between their acidity and the lead in pewter plates.

Cleopatra VII lived closer to the moon landing than to the building of the pyramids.

Answer: Not Bullshit - Cleopatra lived around 2,500 years after the Great Pyramid of Giza was built and about 2,000 years before the first moon landing in 1969.

There are about 3 trillion trees on Earth, while estimates of the number of stars in the Milky Way range from 100 to 400 billion.

Answer: Not Bullshit - There are more trees on Earth than stars in the Milky Way.

Sharks have existed for around 400 million years, whereas trees have only been around for about 350 million years.

Answer: Not Bullshit - Sharks have been around longer than trees.

Turritopsis dohrnii, also known as the "immortal jellyfish," can revert to its juvenile form after reaching adulthood, thus potentially living forever.

Answer: Not Bullshit - There is a species of jellyfish that is considered immortal.

Botanically speaking, bananas qualify as berries, while strawberries do not.

Answer: Not Bullshit - Bananas are berries, but strawberries are not.

The exoplanet WASP-76b, located about 640 light-years from Earth, has such extreme temperatures that iron vaporizes during the day and condenses into iron rain at night.

Answer: Not Bullshit - There is a planet where it rains iron.

Venus takes 243 Earth days to rotate once but only 225 Earth days to orbit the Sun.

Answer: Not Bullshit - A day on Venus is longer than a year on Venus.

The blue whale's heart can weigh as much as a small car and can be heard from a significant distance underwater.

Answer: Not Bullshit - You can hear a blue whale's heartbeat from 2 miles away.

The population of plastic lawn flamingos outnumbers the real flamingo population.

Answer: Not Bullshit - There are more fake flamingos in the world than real ones.

An octopus has three hearts: two pump blood to the gills, while one pumps it to the rest of the body.

Answer: Not Bullshit - An octopus has three hearts.

Archaeologists have found pots of honey in ancient Egyptian tombs that are over 3,000 years old and still perfectly edible.

Answer: Not Bullshit - Honey never spoils.

The Anglo-Zanzibar War of 1896 between the United Kingdom and the Sultanate of Zanzibar is the shortest recorded war, lasting less than an hour.

Answer: Not Bullshit - The shortest war in history lasted 38 minutes.

In 18th-century England, pineapples were so expensive that people would rent them for parties to show off.

Answer: Not Bullshit - Pineapples were once so expensive that they were rented.

Studies have shown that cows form close bonds with certain other cows and can become stressed when separated from them.

Answer: Not Bullshit - Cows have best friends.

Sloths can hold their breath for up to 40 minutes by slowing their heart rate, while dolphins need to surface for air more frequently.

Answer: Not Bullshit - Sloths can hold their breath longer than dolphins.

Due to the expansion of iron in the heat, the Eiffel Tower can grow about 6 inches during warm weather.

Answer: Not Bullshit - The Eiffel Tower can be 15 cm taller during the summer.

Just like Earth has earthquakes, the Moon has quakes known as moonquakes, which are caused by the gravitational pull of the Earth.

Answer: Not Bullshit - The Moon has moonquakes.

There are 293 moons in our solar system, yet our Moon is the only one that has a perfect eclipse.

Answer: Not Bullshit - Our Moon is uniquely positioned to create perfect solar eclipses. The Sun is about 400 times larger than the Moon, but also 400 times farther away, making them appear the same size in the sky. This perfect alignment during a total solar eclipse is due to the precise orbital mechanics of the Earth-Moon-Sun system, a phenomenon not shared by any other moons in our solar system.

Bananas are naturally blue before ripening.

Answer: Bullshit - Bananas are actually green before turning yellow.

Humans can naturally see ultraviolet light.

Answer: Bullshit - Humans cannot see ultraviolet light without special equipment.

Penguins are native to the North Pole.

Answer: Bullshit - Penguins are native to the Southern Hemisphere, primarily Antarctica.

The Eiffel Tower was originally planned to be built in Barcelona.

Answer: Bullshit - The Eiffel Tower was always intended to be built in Paris.

Goldfish can grow to the size of a large dog in the wild.

Answer: Bullshit - Goldfish can grow larger in the wild than in captivity, but not to the size of a large dog.

The Great Wall of China is made of rice and mud.

Answer: Bullshit - The Great Wall is primarily made of stone, brick, tamped earth, wood, and other materials.

There is a species of tree that walks to find sunlight.

Answer: Bullshit - Trees do not move locations; they grow towards sunlight.

Cats can breathe underwater.

Answer: Bullshit - Cats, like most mammals, cannot breathe underwater.

Humans can photosynthesize with enough exposure to sunlight.

Answer: Bullshit - Humans cannot photosynthesize; only plants and some microorganisms can.

Venus has liquid water oceans.

Answer: Bullshit - Venus is extremely hot and has no liquid water; its surface is mostly volcanic rock.

There are no rivers in Antarctica.

Answer: Bullshit - Antarctica does have rivers and lakes beneath its ice sheets.

Humans have the same number of bones as a giraffe.

Answer: Bullshit - Giraffes have the same number of neck vertebrae as humans (seven), but not the same total number of bones.

The Amazon Rainforest produces 50% of the world's oxygen.

Answer: Bullshit - The Amazon contributes significantly to oxygen production, but not 50%; a large portion is absorbed back by the ecosystem.

Dolphins are fish.

Answer: Bullshit - Dolphins are mammals, not fish.

The moon has its own light source.

Answer: Bullshit - The moon reflects light from the sun; it does not produce its own light.

Owls are the only birds that can see the color blue.

Answer: Bullshit - Many birds can see a range of colors, including blue.

Horses can sleep standing up and never lie down.

Answer: Bullshit - Horses can sleep standing up, but they also lie down for deep sleep.

An octopus's tentacles have their own brains.

Answer: Bullshit - An octopus's tentacles have complex nervous systems, but not separate brains.

Cows have more than one stomach.

Answer: Bullshit - Cows have one stomach with four compartments, not multiple stomachs.

The Sahara Desert was once covered in ice.

Answer: Bullshit - The Sahara Desert was once a lush, green area but was never covered in ice.

Animals that lay eggs don't have belly buttons.

Answer: Not Bullshit - Animals that lay eggs, such as birds and reptiles, do not have belly buttons because they do not have an umbilical cord.

Mr. Potato Head was the first toy to be advertised on TV.

Answer: Not Bullshit - Mr. Potato Head was indeed the first toy advertised on television in 1952.

There is a psychological disorder in which patients believe they are a cow.

Answer: Not Bullshit - Boanthropy is a rare psychological disorder where a person believes they are a cow or ox.

Camels have three eyelids.

Answer: Not Bullshit - Camels have three eyelids to protect their eyes from sand and dust.

There is a McDonald's on every continent except Antarctica.

Answer: Not Bullshit - McDonald's has locations on every continent except Antarctica.

Mosquitoes are attracted to people who just ate bananas.

Answer: Bullshit - This claim lacks strong scientific evidence. While certain chemicals might attract mosquitoes, the specific effect of eating bananas is not well-documented.

In South Korea, there is an emergency number to report suspected spies (it's 113!).

Answer: Not Bullshit - South Korea has an emergency number, 113, for reporting suspected spies.

Cats can make more than 100 vocalizations.

Answer: Not Bullshit - Cats can make over 100 different vocal sounds.

Sonic the Hedgehog's full name is Ogilvie Maurice Hedgehog.

Answer: Bullshit - This is a fictional, humorous claim and not officially recognized in Sonic the Hedgehog lore.

The world's termites outweigh the world's humans about 10 to 1.

Answer: Not Bullshit - The biomass of termites is indeed estimated to be greater than that of humans.

Most toilet paper sold in France is pink.

Answer: Not Bullshit - Pink toilet paper is common in France.

The Hawaiian alphabet only has 12 letters.

Answer: Not Bullshit - The Hawaiian alphabet consists of 12 letters: 5 vowels and 7 consonants.

The human nose can remember 50,000 different scents.

Answer: Not Bullshit - The human nose is capable of remembering approximately 50,000 different scents.

Children tend to grow faster in the spring.

Answer: Not Bullshit - Studies have shown that children may experience faster growth rates during the spring season.

Sliced bread was invented a year after the invention of TV.

Answer: Bullshit - Sliced bread was invented in 1928, whereas the first demonstration of television occurred in the late 1920s. They were invented around the same time, but not exactly one year apart.

If you keep a goldfish in a dark room, it will eventually turn white.

Answer: Not Bullshit - Goldfish can lose their color and turn white if kept in the dark for extended periods.

Bullfrogs do not sleep.

Answer: Not Bullshit - Bullfrogs have been found to exhibit periods of restful inactivity but do not undergo sleep as we understand it.

A snail breathes through its foot.

Answer: Not Bullshit - Some snails have a breathing hole located on their foot.

Fish cough.

Answer: Not Bullshit - Fish can expel particles and debris from their gills in a manner similar to coughing.

It took the creator of the Rubik's Cube one month to solve the cube after he created it.

Answer: Not Bullshit - Ernő Rubik, the creator of the Rubik's Cube, took about a month to solve his own invention.

Japanese square watermelons aren't edible. They are purely ornamental.

Answer: Not Bullshit - Japanese square watermelons are grown to be ornamental and are often not fully ripe, making them inedible.

An ant's sense of smell is stronger than a dog's.

Answer: Not Bullshit - Ants have a highly developed sense of smell, which is essential for communication and finding food, and in some ways, it can be more acute than a dog's.

Tigers have striped skin, not just striped fur. The stripes are like fingerprints—no two tigers have the same pattern.

Answer: Not Bullshit - Tigers' stripes are indeed present on their skin, and each tiger's stripe pattern is unique.

Elephants are the only mammal that can't jump.

Answer: Not Bullshit - Due to their size and structure, elephants are unable to jump.

Alligators will give manatees the right of way if they are swimming near each other.

Answer: Not Bullshit - Alligators have been observed giving manatees the right of way in water, likely due to manatees' peaceful nature and protected status.

Canned baked beans aren't baked, but stewed.

Answer: Not Bullshit - Canned baked beans are typically stewed, not baked, during the canning process.

Despite its hump, camels have straight spines.

Answer: Not Bullshit - Camels have straight spines; the hump is a fatty deposit and does not affect the spine's alignment.

Sunsets on Mars are blue.

Answer: Not Bullshit - Due to the scattering of light by the Martian atmosphere, sunsets on Mars appear blue.

Digging a hole to China is actually possible if you start in Argentina.

Answer: Bullshit - While the idea of digging a hole to the opposite side of the Earth is a common saying, it is not practically possible due to the Earth's structure and core.

Mosquitoes have 47 teeth.

Answer: Bullshit - Mosquitoes do not have teeth. They have a proboscis, a long, needle-like structure used to pierce the skin and draw blood.

A quarter of the bones in your body are in your feet.

Answer: Not Bullshit - Each foot has 26 bones, so together, the feet contain 52 bones, which is about a quarter of the 206 bones in the human body.

Brain waves can be used to power an electric train.

Answer: Bullshit - While brain waves can be detected and used for various control interfaces, they do not generate sufficient power to run an electric train.

The Boston Marathon didn't allow female runners until 1972.

Answer: Not Bullshit - The Boston Marathon officially allowed female runners to compete starting in 1972.

Pigs can get sunburned.

Answer: Not Bullshit - Pigs can get sunburned, especially those with lighter skin.

A one-day weather forecast requires about 10 billion math calculations.

Answer: Not Bullshit - Modern weather forecasting involves complex models that require billions of calculations to predict weather accurately.

"Bluetooth" technology was named after a 10th-century king, King Harald "Bluetooth" Gormsson. He united Denmark and Norway, just like the technology united computers and cell phones.

Answer: Not Bullshit - Bluetooth technology is indeed named after King Harald "Bluetooth" Gormsson, who united Denmark and Norway.

There are 19 different animal shapes in the animal cracker zoo.

Answer: Bullshit - There are actually 54 different animal shapes in Barnum's Animal Crackers.

Hart Island is the final burial place for over a million of New York City's unclaimed bodies.

Answer: Not Bullshit - Hart Island serves as a potter's field, where over a million unclaimed or unidentified New Yorkers have been buried.

There's a river called "Big Ugly Creek" in West Virginia.

Answer: Not Bullshit - There is indeed a river named "Big Ugly Creek" in West Virginia.

You share your birthday with at least 9 million other people in the world.

Answer: Bullshit(Sort of) - Statistically, you share your birthday with approximately 19 million other people worldwide.

No piece of A4 paper can be folded more than 7 times.

Answer: Bullshit - While it's difficult, it has been proven possible to fold a piece of paper more than 7 times under specific conditions, such as using a larger sheet of paper and different techniques.

In Slovakia, they have Christmas carp that live in the bathtub for a few days before they are eaten.

Answer: Not Bullshit - In Slovakia and some other Central European countries, it is a tradition to keep a carp in the bathtub before preparing it for Christmas dinner.

The state of Ohio gives out different colored license plates for those with a DUI conviction.

Answer: Not Bullshit - Ohio issues yellow license plates with red letters for individuals convicted of a DUI.

People don't sneeze in their sleep due to their brain shutting down the reflex.

Answer: Not Bullshit - The brain suppresses the sneeze reflex during sleep, so people generally don't sneeze while sleeping.

Alaska has more caribou than people.

Answer: Not Bullshit - Alaska has a large caribou population, often outnumbering the human population.

Oysters can change from one gender to another (and back again).

Answer: Not Bullshit - Oysters can indeed change their gender multiple times throughout their lives.

Dead people can get goosebumps.

Answer: Not Bullshit - Goosebumps can occur after death due to muscle contractions as the body goes through rigor mortis.

A ten-gallon hat holds less than one gallon of liquid.

Answer: Not Bullshit - Despite its name, a ten-gallon hat holds less than one gallon of liquid.

The average raindrop falls at 7 mph.

Answer: Not Bullshit - The average raindrop falls at a speed of about 7 miles per hour.

Guy Fawkes is the reason men are called "guys."

Answer: Not Bullshit - The term "guy" comes from Guy Fawkes, the man behind the Gunpowder Plot of 1605 and the mask portrayed in the movie "V for Vendetta". The term evolved over time to refer to men in general.

Lizards communicate by doing push-ups.

Answer: Not Bullshit - Some lizards use push-up displays as a form of communication, often to show dominance or attract mates.

A giant squid has eyes the size of a volleyball.

Answer: Not Bullshit - The eyes of a giant squid can be as large as a volleyball, around 10 inches in diameter.

The average American will eat 35,000 cookies in their lifetime.

Answer: Not Bullshit - It's estimated that the average American consumes around 35,000 cookies over their lifetime.

Banks have therapists known as "wealth psychologists" who help clients who are unable to mentally cope with their immense wealth.

Answer: Not Bullshit - Some banks and financial institutions employ wealth psychologists to help clients manage the psychological aspects of having great wealth.

Dogs have been banned from Antarctica since April 1994 out of concern that dogs might spread diseases to seals.

Answer: Not Bullshit - Dogs were banned from Antarctica by the Antarctic Treaty in 1994 to prevent the potential spread of diseases to native seal populations.

Smelling apples or bananas can help you lose weight.

Answer: Bullshit - There is no scientific evidence that smelling apples or bananas has a significant impact on weight loss.

In 1998, more than 50% of Iceland's population believed in the existence of elves.

Answer: Not Bullshit - Surveys in Iceland have shown that a significant portion of the population believes in the possibility of elves.

Beavers were once the size of bears.

Answer: Not Bullshit - Prehistoric beavers, such as Castoroides, were as large as bears, growing up to 8 feet long.

A pigeon's feathers weigh more than their bones.

Answer: Not Bullshit - Pigeons, like many birds, have hollow bones that make their feathers weigh more than their skeletal structure.

A crocodile can't move its tongue.

Answer: Not Bullshit - Crocodiles have a membrane that holds their tongue in place on the roof of their mouth, preventing it from moving.

Honeybees navigate using the sun as their compass.

Answer: Not Bullshit - Honeybees use the position of the sun to navigate and find their way back to the hive.

If you sneeze traveling 60 mph, your eyes are closed for an average of 50 feet.

Answer: Not Bullshit - When sneezing at 60 mph, your eyes can be closed for about 50 feet, though this can vary slightly.

Hawaii is the only state to grow coffee commercially.

Answer: Not Bullshit - Hawaii is the only U.S. state where coffee is grown commercially.

The square dance is the official state dance of Washington.

Answer: Not Bullshit - The official state dance of Washington is the square dance. However, this is also the case for 23 other states.

When dinosaurs roamed the earth, volcanos were erupting on the moon.

Answer: Bullshit - There is no evidence to suggest that there were active volcanoes on the moon during the time of the dinosaurs.

The only letters that don't appear on the periodic table are J and Q.

Answer: Not Bullshit - The letters J and Q do not appear on the periodic table of elements.

At birth, a baby panda is smaller than a mouse.

Answer: Not Bullshit - Newborn baby pandas are very small, weighing about 100 grams, which is indeed smaller than a typical mouse.

In 1923, a jockey suffered a fatal heart attack mid-race. His horse finished and won the race, making him the first and only jockey to win a race after death.

Answer: Not Bullshit - In 1923, jockey Frank Hayes died of a heart attack during a race, but his horse crossed the finish line first, making him the only jockey to win posthumously.

In order to protect themselves from poachers, African elephants have been evolving without tusks.

Answer: Not Bullshit - Due to heavy poaching, there is an increase in the number of tuskless elephants as a form of evolutionary response.

In order to keep Nazis away, a Polish doctor faked a typhus outbreak that saved more than 8,000 people.

Answer: Not Bullshit - Polish doctor Eugene Lazowski created a fake typhus epidemic during World War II, which saved thousands of people from being sent to Nazi camps.

The spiked dog collar was invented by the ancient Greeks to protect their dogs from wolf attacks.

Answer: Not Bullshit - The spiked dog collar was designed by ancient Greeks to protect dogs' necks from wolf bites.

German chocolate cake is named after an American baker named Samuel German.

Answer: Not Bullshit - German chocolate cake is named after Samuel German, who developed a type of dark baking chocolate for the Baker's Chocolate Company.

During World War II, Germany planned to collapse the British economy by dropping millions of counterfeit bills over London.

Answer: Not Bullshit - Operation Bernhard was a German plan to destabilize the British economy by flooding it with counterfeit bills during World War II.

The youngest pope in history was Pope Benedict IX. He is also the only person to have been the pope more than once.

Answer: Not Bullshit - Pope Benedict IX became pope in his teens and held the papacy three separate times.

The tallest man in recorded history was 8'11.

Answer: Not Bullshit - Robert Wadlow, the tallest man in recorded history, was 8 feet 11 inches tall.

IKEA is an acronym that stands for Ingvar Kamprad Elmtaryd Agunnaryd: the founder's name, the farm where he grew up, and his hometown.

Answer: Not Bullshit - IKEA is an acronym for Ingvar Kamprad Elmtaryd Agunnaryd, which refers to the founder's name, his family's farm, and his hometown.

There is a town in Nebraska called Monowi with a population of one. The only resident is a woman who serves as mayor, bartender, and librarian.

Answer: Not Bullshit - Monowi, Nebraska, is indeed known for having a population of one. Elsie Eiler serves as the town's mayor, bartender, and librarian.

The unique smell of rain actually comes from plant oils, bacteria, and ozone.

Answer: Not Bullshit - The smell of rain, called petrichor, comes from oils released by plants, actinobacteria, and ozone.

Vanilla flavoring is sometimes made with a liquid secreted from beavers' castor glands.

Answer: Not Bullshit - Castoreum, a secretion from beavers' castor glands, has been used as a flavoring in food, including vanilla, though it is rare today.

The oldest unopened bottle of wine was found in a Roman tomb and is more than 1,650 years old.

Answer: Not Bullshit - The Speyer wine bottle, found in a Roman tomb, is over 1,650 years old and is considered the oldest known unopened bottle of wine.

In 2016, Domino's tested pizza delivery via reindeer in Japan.

Answer: Not Bullshit - Domino's Japan did test pizza delivery via reindeer in 2016.

Helen Keller is related to Robert E. Lee — her paternal grandfather was his second cousin.

Answer: Not Bullshit - Helen Keller was related to Robert E. Lee through her paternal grandfather, who was Lee's second cousin.

Starfish don't have blood. They circulate nutrients by using seawater in their vascular system.

Answer: Not Bullshit - Starfish use seawater in their water vascular system to circulate nutrients and oxygen.

Adult cats only meow at humans, not other cats.

Answer: Not Bullshit - Adult cats primarily use meowing to communicate with humans; they use other vocalizations and body language to communicate with other cats.

Video games have been found to be more effective at battling depression than some kinds of therapy.

Answer: Not Bullshit - Some studies have shown that certain video games can be effective in reducing symptoms of depression, sometimes more so than traditional therapy.

It's a common belief in Russia that eating ice cream will keep you warm.

Answer: Not Bullshit - It is a common belief in Russia that eating ice cream in cold weather can help the body adjust to the cold.

Underneath the streets of Beijing, there are around a million people who live in nuclear bunkers.

Answer: Not Bullshit - Due to housing shortages, it's estimated that about a million people live in former nuclear bunkers beneath Beijing.

A study from Harvard University finds that having no friends can be just as deadly as smoking. Both affect levels of a blood-clotting protein.

Answer: Not Bullshit - Studies, including those from Harvard, have found that social isolation can have severe health impacts, comparable to the effects of smoking.

All new FBI special agents and intelligence analysts are required to visit the United States Holocaust Memorial Museum.

Answer: Not Bullshit - It is a requirement for new FBI special agents and intelligence analysts to visit the United States Holocaust Memorial Museum as part of their training.

Garlic is known to attract leeches.

Answer: Not Bullshit - Garlic can attract leeches, contrary to the popular belief that it repels them.

The gold in Tutankhamun's tomb had been stolen from the tombs of other pharaohs.

Answer: Bullshit - There is no evidence that the gold in Tutankhamun's tomb was stolen from other tombs.

New York City mob boss Vincent Gigante used to avoid arrest by wandering around in his bathrobe to convince the police he was insane.

Answer: Not Bullshit - Vincent Gigante, a New York City mob boss, feigned insanity by wandering around in his bathrobe to avoid arrest and prosecution.

Johnny Cash once got into a fistfight with Colonel Sanders over a sports game.

Answer: Bullshit - There is no record of Johnny Cash getting into a fistfight with Colonel Sanders.

Bubble wrap was originally invented to be a kind of plastic wallpaper.

Answer: Not Bullshit - Bubble wrap was invented in 1957 by engineers Alfred Fielding and Marc Chavannes as a type of textured wallpaper.

Jeannette Rankin was elected to the House of Representatives four years before women had won the right to vote.

Answer: Not Bullshit - Jeannette Rankin was elected to the U.S. House of Representatives in 1916, four years before the 19th Amendment granted women the right to vote.

In the Netherlands' version of Sesame Street, there's a bluebird named Pino instead of Big Bird. Pino was later introduced as Big Bird's cousin.

Answer: Not Bullshit - The Dutch version of Sesame Street features a bluebird named Pino, who is presented as Big Bird's cousin.

The same molecule that makes chicken taste like chicken can also be found in ground-up oyster shells.

Answer: Bullshit - There is no evidence supporting that the flavor molecule for chicken is found in oyster shells.

Portions of the Bible have been translated into more than 3,000 languages, including fictional languages

Answer: Not Bullshit - Portions of the Bible have been translated into over 3,000 languages, including fictional ones like Elvish, Klingon, and Na'vi.

The longest hiccup in history lasted for more than 60 years after it began.

Answer: Not Bullshit - Charles Osborne holds the record for the longest hiccup spell, which lasted for 68 years from 1922 to 1990.

The first bird to ever use an Xbox controller was a Kea called Parau.

Answer: Bullshit - There is no verified record of a bird named Parau using an Xbox controller.

England's biggest horticultural export is the fig.

Answer: Bullshit - England's largest horticultural exports are generally considered to be plants, seeds, and flowers, not figs.

Prince Phillip is widely credited with the invention of the party popper.

Answer: Bullshit - The party popper was invented by Englishman Tom Smith in the 19th century, not Prince Phillip.

Thyme is technically a tree.

Answer: Bullshit - Thyme is an herb, not a tree.

By definition, a snake's body is a limb.

Answer: Bullshit - A snake's body is not defined as a limb.

The roller coaster was invented during the Hundred Years' War as a way of launching supplies across rivers.

Answer: Bullshit - Roller coasters were not invented during the Hundred Years' War; they originated in the 17th century in Russia.

The toenail of your little toe is called the 'spungle.'

Answer: Bullshit - There is no medical term "spungle" for the toenail of the little toe.

Courgette is actually the feminine noun of cucumber.

Answer: Bullshit - Courgette is the British term for zucchini, not a feminine noun for cucumber.

The first video ever uploaded to YouTube had to be taken down in 2016 for violating their Terms of Service.

Answer: Bullshit - The first video, "Me at the zoo," uploaded by YouTube co-founder Jawed Karim, is still available on the platform.

There is a nerveless area of skin half the size of a playing card on the top of your foot. Your brain compensates for it.

Answer: Bullshit - There is no known nerveless area of skin on the top of the foot.

The biggest arms manufacturer in the world is Hasbro.

Answer: Bullshit - Hasbro is a toy company, not an arms manufacturer. The largest arms manufacturers include companies like Lockheed Martin and Boeing.

By weight, bay leaves contain more caffeine than coffee beans. They are used to make a stimulating tea in Morocco.

Answer: Bullshit - Bay leaves do not contain caffeine, and there is no record of them being used to make a stimulating tea in Morocco.

Vikings fired flaming arrows at boats carrying the dead. They would sink them by running them over with a larger boat.

Answer: Bullshit - There is no historical evidence supporting this claim about Viking funeral practices.

There is a 'Buzzy Bee' still at the top of Mt Everest, left there by Edmund Hillary.

Answer: Bullshit - There is no verified record of a 'Buzzy Bee' toy being left on Mt. Everest by Edmund Hillary.

Originally the Fonz was going to wear a leather vest but the popularity of the Village People made them switch to a jacket.

Answer: Bullshit - There is no evidence that the decision for the Fonz to wear a leather jacket was influenced by the Village People.

Thank you for purchasing our book. We hope you found it interesting and enjoyable.

We've researched extensively to provide fun facts that are often misunderstood. Despite our best efforts in self-editing, with over 200 pages and hundreds of entries, some errors may have slipped through. Professional editing wasn't feasible for us.

Instead of leaving a negative review, please consider giving us a chance to correct any mistakes. Send your feedback to bsornbs@gmail.com, and we'll update the book accordingly and credit you. If you have verifiable facts to share, we'd love to include them and acknowledge your contribution in future editions.

We have more category-specific books in the works and hope you'll join us for those too.

Thank you again!

-The BSORNBS Team

www.ingramcontent.com/pod-product-compliance
Lightning Source LLC
Chambersburg PA
CBHW070827250726
48662CB00003B/1121